The Doctor of Arts Degree: Re-Assessing Teaching and Research Priorities

Edited by

ANNE PAOLUCCI

OUNCIL on NATIONAL LITERATURES

P.O. BOX 81 • WHITESTONE, NEW YORK 11357

ISSN: 1043-8343

ISBN: 0-918680-42-5

CNL/WORLD REPORT

NEW SERIES: IV (1988)

==

*A Forum for scholars concerned with comparative study of
the established, emergent, and neglected national literatures
that make up the written and oral artistic legacy of the diverse
contemporary peoples of the world.*

==

Contents

THE PUBLICATION OF THIS VOLUME OF **CNL/WR** WAS MADE POSSIBLE BY A GENEROUS GRANT FROM ST. JOHN'S UNIVERSITY

Editor's Preface

ANNE PAOLUCCI
President, CNL
Editor, CNL/World Report

About two years ago, an idea which had been persistently and frustratingly evasive for months and years began to germinate and finally surfaced as a real possibility. Since my appointment as director of the Doctor of Arts Degree Program in English at St. John's University, I had wanted to reach out to other directors and heads of similar programs in universities throughout the county; my first efforts—in the mid-eighties—were not very successful. The full extent of our individual isolation was brought home to me when a colleague (director of a D.A. Program at another institution) called to ask how we went about placing our graduates. I told him we did not really have that problem, since most of our students were already teaching and only a small minority were between jobs. It struck us both at the time that there were many things about our programs that were different enough to give us pause. I decided to try once again to reach as many directors of D.A. programs as I could—this time with a view toward airing our problems and reviewing the history of our programs at a public meeting of some kind. I also felt strongly that whatever surfaced at such a meeting would prove invaluable toward reviewing programs nationally; and with that in mind I arranged—as President of the Council on National Literatures, an affiliated association of the Modern Language Association—to make available two sessions, back to back, at the December 1988 MLA meeting in New Orleans. I was delighted to find that this time around there was a great deal of interest on the part of D.A. directors to share ideas and a common desire for long-range networking and possibly a publication similar to *ADE, College English*, etc. in which matters of interest to us, as Directors of D.A. degree programs, could be shared.

This issue of *CNL/World Report* (one of two annual publications put out by the Council on National Literatures) is the tangible result of the memorable conference of December 1988—the first of its kind in this decade. In the present volume those who participated in the conference are represented with papers in most cases somewhat longer than the original oral presentations. I am personally delighted that this important volume has also been made accessible (through a generous grant from St. John's University) to educators here and abroad.

Finally, I wish to stress, as a D.A. Director, the urgent need for reassessing the priorities in teaching education: the older degrees have their place and fill a real need; but in the case of the Ph.D., the demand has diminished dramatically while the supply remains pretty much the same. We all know what has happened in recent years: qualified Ph.D. degree holders have left the academy for jobs in other fields. Some of our best educational potential in other words has been lost to the academy. Perhaps this will serve as a positive force in the long run. Right now, however, what is devastatingly clear is that the current crop of Ph.D.s—newly-emergent "researchers"— simply cannot cope with the increasing demand for basic training, in many cases even pre-college training, in "core" college courses. Even when dealing with elective courses, many young teachers with recently acquired Ph.D.s find themselves talking to the walls of the classroom, often not even realizing how great the gap is between intention to communicate and what actually reaches students.

What the D.A. has done, among other things, and without sacrificing in any way the rich content-oriented materials of graduate study, is to give the classroom experience first priority in the order of things: research and lectures must be "translated" in many different ways to reach students of different levels. Lectures as such are replaced with—ideally—roundtable formats, open-ended dialogues, in which the instructor serves as a moderator, skillfully putting forward the Socratic questions, creating debates among the students, using every tool of rhetoric to prove that learning is a *process* as well as an *end product*.

I wish to thank all the participants in our conference who helped to make this publication its "end product"—though certainly not an "end" to this interesting and vital discussion of the future of our profession.

Why Doctor of Arts, Now?

WILLARD GINGERICH
Associate Dean of Graduate School
St. John's University

The higher education teacher crisis of the 21st century is already upon us, warns Michael Sovern, president of Columbia University: "At Columbia, nearly half of the tenured professors in the arts and sciences will retire in the 1990's. Colleges and universities all over the country are facing a massive wave of retirements." So it would seem. "By the year 2000," Sovern concludes, "many of our great teachers will have retired, and too many of those with the potential to become great teachers will have been lured into far more lucrative careers in business and the professions."

But certainly we are faced with something more than a question of money, however influential and real that question may be, and it is emphatically real. The hue and cry after the professoriate, however, from Alan Bloom to Charles Sykes, in the media and popular press shows little awareness of, concern for, or inclination to sympathize with the financial disparities that Sovern sketches out ("My son commanded a higher salary when he began at a prestigious law firm than I did when I became dean of the law school.") The attacks are too wild and outrageous ("The professors—working steadily and systematically—have destroyed the university as a center of learning and have desolated higher education, which no longer is higher or much of an education": Sykes), or too measured and reasonable ("Too seldom is collegiate teaching viewed for what it is: The business of the business—the activity that is central to all colleges and universities": Pew Charitable Trust Report on College Teaching), to be answered simply with the equation: Higher salaries = better profs.

The doctor of arts programs, twenty years after their introduction, are still the most impressive response to the still pressing problem of priorities in American higher education generally and the need to restructure the education of college teachers in particular. The doctor of arts degree originated in a critical evaluation of graduate education which began in the late 1960's, and focused on the training received by those who sought positions in undergraduate teaching programs. It had become too painfully obvious that students prepared in traditional Ph.D. programs knew little about teaching, were neither trained to teach nor inclined to learn, and apparently obtained their major satisfaction and fulfillment only through research and writing. Yet, most graduates of these traditional and increasingly specialized programs eventually found themselves teaching in undergraduate classrooms where they generally muddled through to some kind of competency while pursuing tenure.

It would seem the problem has not gone away: "Our new Ph.D.s do not think of themselves as newly-minted teachers; they consider themselves to be economists, chemists, botanists and historians. Indeed, for many, the characterization 'teacher' would be an insult. Yet, ironically , these young graduates will spend most of their careers teaching, not conducting research, and it is the students or parents, and not research sponsors, who will pick up the cost of their paychecks." This from a December 1988 address to the Council of Graduate Schools by Craufurd Goodwin, James B. Duke Professor of Economics and former Dean of Graduate School, Duke University. And from the recent Pew Report: "American colleges and universities can no longer afford the belief that teaching is simple and easily achieved. It demands artful and imaginative presentation as well as the ability to establish a classroom environment enabling students to construct knowledge plausibly and sensibly." The report goes on to encourage a period of apprenticeship during which graduate students would regularly observe seasoned teachers, then teach and design course syllabi under close supervision and with periodic critiques. Of course, the report notes, few universities provide such guidance and preparation.

The D.A. or "teaching doctorate," which had been discussed

as an alternative doctoral degree for decades, came of age
in 1967 when Carnegie-Mellon opened the first D.A. programs
in English, mathematics, history and fine arts. Within three
years, in 1970, the Council of Graduate Schools recommended
the establishment of programs leading to the degree of Doctor
of Arts to prepare students for effective teaching. By 1988,
over 1500 D.A.s had been awarded, 700 (47%) since 1979,
predominantly in English, chemistry, mathematics, biology and
history. While the number of institutions offering the degree
(twenty-four in 1988) has remained fairly constant since the
mid-seventies, the number of graduates has increased by 52%
between 1980 and 1988, with an 18.6% increase between 1987
and 1988 alone. The dozen larger programs providing
employment information in the 1988 survey (by Dean David
L. Wheeler of Ball State University) report that 92% of their
June graduates held positions at the time of graduation.

In its "Supplemental Statement on the Doctor of Arts
Degree," the Council of Graduate Schools defines the goal
of D.A. programs as the creation of "teaching scholars" and
attributes to such scholars the following characteristics "which
make them more valuable at the outset to undergraduate
institutions and to those whom they teach":

> [Teaching scholars] will be student-oriented, and the main
> thrust of [their] scholarship will be in the teaching-learning
> process, in the dissemination of knowledge. [They]will
> be interested in a broad humanistic approach to the
> instruction of those who as citizens must deal in daily
> life with a broad spectrum of problems and human
> resources and weaknesses. [They] seek to integrate
> knowledge at the undergraduate level of teaching—not
> to specialize and fragment what the students learn.
> Although effective college teachers are appreciative of the
> depth of scholarship exemplified by their more specialized
> colleagues and are able to apply the results of their
> research, they usually teach a broader range of courses
> in the undergraduate college. They must possess research
> skills sufficient for maintaining their personal scholarship,

which may be reflected in publications and participation in learned societies and organizations; however, the teaching scholar's main purpose will be the effective application of research to teaching. (Supplemental Statement on the Doctor of Arts Degree. Council of Graduate Schools, 1972)

In its original 1970 statement the Council emphasized that the Ph.D. should remain the terminal research degree in American higher education; the D.A. would emphasize research *and* teaching within a given subject area. As it evolved in the 1970's, the Doctor of Arts Degree was designed not to replace, but to parallel, existing Ph.D. programs and oriented towards developing teacher competence in a broad subject matter area. To assure a more comprehensive coverage, broad course selection across several disciplines was recommended. This emphasis then transcended the specialization found within most Ph.D. programs—and still does, in spite of the recent efforts of some Ph.D. programs to alter themselves into the shape of the D.A. There was also a call for foreign language and research tools that would be functional rather than nominal, a research component that would have practical applicability in the classroom, a supervised internship or its equivalent to improve teaching, and finally a less specialized comprehensive exam than was generally found within Ph.D. programs.

A primary difference between the D.A. and the Ph.D. is the purpose and scope of the research component in the respective programs. As do all doctoral programs, the D.A. requires that the student develop a strong research capability. However, in the D.A. program this capability has a focus and intensity different from that for the Ph.D.; while the latter results in a dissertation which presumably demonstrates the discovery of new knowledge, within the D.A. program the research component leads to an enhancement of scholarly knowledge and its application in the classroom. Early D.A. granting institutions stressed the need for a problem or theme concentration in those degree programs based on two or more disciplines. They also called for instruction and experience in the methodologies of the particular disciplines as well as one of more courses focusing on instruction or curricular problems.

In 1971 the Regents of the State of New York authorized the granting of the doctor of arts degree in New York. The guidelines adopted by New York State incorporated most of the features outlined by the Council of Graduate Schools and previous D.A. granting institutions. In the State's revised guidelines the Regents announced that "the Doctor of Arts degree presumes more comprehensive knowledge and broader course work than is customarily the case with the Ph.D. combined with the mastery of a discipline."

In addition to the earlier requirements New York State called for competence in communication skills and stressed the need to provide a broad graduate education not only for teachers but for people in business, government agencies, and other areas where such knowledge would be useful.

The New York State guidelines for the D.A. require that a degree recipient demonstrate:

- comprehensive knowledge as demonstrated by written and oral examinations;

- skills appropriate to the practice of a particular profession;

- competence in the methods and practice of research, as evidenced by a research essay;

- competence in communications skills;

- an appropriate practicum or its equivalent.

Currently, six institutions offer the Doctor of Arts degree in New York State: Adelphi University (Speech and Pathology and Audiology), New York University (Arts Professions), SUNY at Albany (Humanistic Studies and English), SUNY at Stony Brook (Foreign Language Instruction), Syracuse University (Foreign Languages), and St. John's University (English and Modern World History).

Obviously, not all D.A. programs have thrived. There is still too much misperception and confusion about the nature and purpose of the degree; standards and programs vary. Some, such as the English and Modern World History programs at St. John's University, are more demanding than Ph.D. programs, in the number of required credits but especially in the many-faceted approach to traditional subjects, issues and authors. Others seem to see the D.A. as little more than an M.Phil. degree. New York has set an example by defining clearly and rigorously the doctoral level expectations of any D.A. program in the state.

Just as obviously, the doctor of arts provides an answer to the teaching crisis of the professoriate so much urged upon us. Its insistence on preparing teachers in the discipline rather than in educational theory anticipates the national consensus in that direction (beginning in 1990 no secondary teacher will be certified in Texas without at least a bachelor's degree in the subject he or she will teach). The serious attention given to the discipline and art of teaching in these programs corrects the myopic, self-defeating career image among Ph.D. graduates so lamented by Dean Goodwin.

During the next decade when the educational establishment will introduce far-reaching changes in its curricular structures, a need long recognized and discussed and already in the process of implementation, the scholar teacher with the Doctor of Arts degree will be ideally prepared to participate and lead in this development. The degree's broad focus, solid research training, emphasis on interdisciplinarity, concern with cultural pluralism and innovative teaching will give its holders a decided advantage for leadership roles. Indeed the holder of the D.A. will in many respects be prepared to embrace if not embody the focus on excellence in education which has again become a national concern and to assume a leadership role in introducing changes, more so than the holders of the more narrowly specialized Ph.D. or the often non-discipline based Ed.D. The D.A. will also play an important role in forging institutional and instructional links between secondary schools and universities, which has been long overdue and is necessary for an improvement of education at both levels.

The question is not Why the D.A. Now? but Why has it taken so long?

How the History of American Graduate Education Favored The Genesis of the Doctor of Arts Degree

JO ANNE K. HECKER
Associate Dean, Graduate School
University of Miami

Since the introduction of the Ph.D. in 1861, American graduate education has accepted that degree form as the major credential for college and university faculty. Many educators disparage its value, however, because of the overriding emphasis placed on a research component when so few of its recipients continue as scholars. Yet accrediting associations continue to promote the degree's market value; and university administrators increasingly employ it as a selective screening device for college faculty whose primary tasks will be teaching.

An assortment of alternate graduate degrees emphasizing teacher training has appeared throughout the last fifty years. Most were master's or intermediate-level degrees. But these degrees, which arose in response to criticisms of the research-oriented Ph.D., never earned the respect that a doctorate might. Some Ph.D. programs even added teaching tracks, but many faculty were suspicious of tampering with the research degree.

During the late 1960s the Doctor of Arts degree appeared as a model doctoral program specifically to train college teachers. Carnegie-Mellon University introduced the degree, and the Carnegie Corporation of New York supported the effort. Prominent community college groups, the American Association of State Colleges and Universities, and the Council of Graduate Schools in the United States endorsed the degree. A decade later the Doctor of Arts degree existed at twenty-five institutions in twenty-seven fields of study, and by 1988—

two decades later—twenty-four institutions, (although the group differs somewhat) still offer the program.

The purpose of this report is to present an historical summary of conditions that fostered the emergence of the Doctor of Arts degree. Interestingly, approximately three hundred years of American higher education preceded its appearance. To understand why this new doctoral form appeared when it did, an evolutionary review of American education is appropriate.

The first two hundred years in the history of American graduate degrees were doctorless ones. Actually, the early American college before the Civil War commanded very little prestige in either rural or urban areas (Veysey 6). Only a handful of American colleges strived for "university" status. Conservative, aged college presidents at leading institutions, a devotion to a classical curriculum, clergymen as educational leaders, and a guardedness about vocationalism describe the realities of American higher education in 1850. Most attempts at academic reform in the first half of the nineteenth century were quietly ignored in the East or dispersed to the Midwest (Storr; Veysey; Rudolph 118).

While the population soared 23 percent in the decade of the 1870s, attendance at twenty of the oldest leading colleges rose but 3.5 percent (U.S. Commissioner of Education). About this time a new group of academic leaders edged into prominence propelled by jolts of "newly released wealth and an awareness of static or declining college enrollment" (Veysey 10). Many college administrators sensed the potential growth and were led and encouraged by some of the younger charismatic college presidents who took office at the time, such as Eliot of Harvard, Gilman of Johns Hopkins, and White of Cornell.

One static component of the American structure was its graduate degree system. Master's degrees from American colleges, along with baccalaureate degrees, replicated their English models. Awarded in America since the early 1600s, the master's degree was often attained for little more than payment of the prescribed fees. A few ineffective attempts to strengthen and elevate the master's degree were made in the early nineteenth century. The University of Michigan in 1858, however, became the first major university to rehabilitate the master's degree, requiring at least one year of graduate study beyond the bachelor's degree, along with proper examinations.

Thus, for two centuries American colleges existed, but exerted little cultural influence on the population as a whole. The degree structure consisted of bachelor's and master's degrees. Americans established few universities; those that emerged tended to be small and different from each other. Meanwhile, European universities stirred with new, lively ideas—especially in the sciences. And many American scholars who sought academia's loftier levels traveled to Europe to study (Veysey).

By the end of the Civil War, American higher education, having existed over two hundred years, was languishing for lack of prestige, practical relevance, and financial support. The term "university" also began to appear more frequently at this time although the definition of such an American institution was by no means uniform or clear.

Modeling the educational system after a European one gained favor. In 1861 Yale offered the first research doctorate, the Ph.D., and in 1876, Johns Hopkins opened its doors as a strictly graduate institution. Yale's decision to offer the doctorate was made, in part, to keep American students at home as more and more of them, particularly in the sciences, traveled abroad to German universities (Veysey 10). The year 1861 marks a turning point.

During the last half of the nineteenth century, Clark University, Catholic University, the University of Chicago, and Harvard were among the first to offer the Ph.D., closely followed by the Universities of Michigan, Wisconsin, Nebraska, and Kansas (Spurr 118). The Johns Hopkins model, amply funded, set a high tone for doctoral education. Distinguished faculty, graduate student fellowships, publication of journals, and the "seminar" teaching model set an academic standard that created "virtual missionaries" of Johns Hopkins graduates (Storr 43). Several annual meetings of the Federation of Graduate clubs set forth strict uniform requirements for the

Doctor of Philosophy degree, and these rules were generally adhered to by all Ph.D.-granting institutions. (Spurr 118)

Between 1875 and 1900, Hollis states, graduate instruction in the leading universities was in the hands of staff members, a majority of whom did not have the Ph.D. degree themselves (Hollis 18). Visiting professors were often used to fill the gaps which existed. Hyder, in his biography of Harvard English literature scholar, George Lyman Kittredge, repeats the famous answer Kittredge often gave to the question of why he did not take his Ph.D. degree: "Who would have examined me?" (Kittredge, on several occasions, labeled the quote as untrue, saying, "I never had time to earn a Ph.D. degree. Besides, I always told my students I probably couldn't pass the exam [!]" (Hyder 185).

Research activities in universities rose to greater prominence following the advent of the American Ph.D. and the establishment of the Johns Hopkins University. Ultimately, during the first half of the twentieth century, the Ph.D. became the degree to possess for professional advancement in all academic careers. Storr, reflecting on the meaning of degrees, concludes that the Ph.D. has been less villain than victim. The importance of the degree "was obscured when a false emphasis upon degrees as hallmarks of mind (or worse, of personal merit) worked to make having a degree an end in itself." (Storr 82) William James wrote in 1903 of the Ph.D. "octopus," and Barzun (1945) deplored the over-emphasis on the Ph.D. as a symbol of attainment in academia, as well as the degree's use as a professional appointment screening device.

The phenomenal growth of the Ph.D. in the United States bears note. In the year 1908, 394 Ph.D.'s were awarded by 38 institutions. In 1920, 615 Ph.D.'s were granted. In 1950, 6,420 Ph.D.'s were issued and in 1971, 15,000 Ph.D.'s were granted by over 240 institutions (Eble 105).

The Ph.D. is, in stated purpose and effect, a research degree. Criticism of the excessive emphasis placed upon Ph.D. research training and the pressure to publish continued unabated for seventy-five years (James; Arrowsmith). Spokesmen from undergraduate institutions contend that Ph.D. holders are required to teach but are often untrained for the task (Cardozier 261).

In truth, the emerging research degree, the Ph.D., lowered the status of the teaching function among the professoriate of American colleges and universities.

> The most profound effect of the increasing emphasis on specialized research was a tendency among scientifically minded professors to ignore the undergraduate college and to place a low value upon this function as teachers . . . . If investigation was the principal aim of the university, then giving one's energy to immature and frequently mediocre students could easily seem an irritating irrelevance. (Veysey 144)

James criticized the degree for being an unnecessary prerequisite to college teaching (James 278). Flexner stated that "the university has sacrificed college teaching at the altar of research" (Flexner 37).

In the 1930's studies showed that few graduate schools accepted any suggestions for curriculum changes and were strongly opposed to planning a new degree with emphasis on college teaching. At a 1948 conference of the National Education Association, a special conference group dealt intensively with the issue of the preparation of college teachers. One important conclusion was:

> Those students who are preparing for college teaching should be afforded somewhat different educational experiences than those who are looking forward to careers in research, industry, governmental service, or other fields. (McDonald and McCaskill 141)

From 1940 to 1965 several conditions "combined to dilute and subordinate undergraduate teaching." These were the rising proportion of college-eligible youth actually attending colleges; advances in the status, prestige, and recognition of the academic profession; the deeper involvement of the faculty member in the local, national, and international setting; and the expanding support from the Federal government for a wide range of research and service activities (Caffrey 33).

Many articles appeared in the 1950s debating the teacher-scholar emphasis in Ph.D. training. Volpe wrote that "the professor cannot successfully fulfill his duties in the classroom without changing from scholar to teacher (Lehrer 314). Dykstra, commenting in 1958 about the "Ph.D. fetish," indicated that:

> The Ph.D. program has about as much relation to classroom competence as a course in bullfighting has to proficiency in agriculture . . . . Sociologists have noted that the ostensible reason for perpetuating practices in a society often are quite different from the real ones. From a college administrator's point of view, the existence of a Ph.D. emphasis has always simplified the task of selecting personnel to fill faculty vacancies. Meaningful evidence of an applicant's ability to perform with competence the duties expected of him is seldom available. Insistence upon persons with a Ph.D. for the job has served to narrow down the field to manageable proportions before the more amorphous, real considerations must be reckoned with . . . . If the acquisition of the Ph.D. is to continue to be the key to academic acceptability for college faculty, the requirements for the degree should be made to bear a more meaningful relationship to the work expected of such professions. (*Ibid.*328)

The anomaly of the Ph.D. remains: top graduate students are selected and trained to do research, then a good portion of them are employed to teach in undergraduate situations, and finally, they are rewarded on the amount and quality of research they do!

Eble confirms the fact that college teachers distrust administrators' pronouncements about concern for teaching because "the reward system is out of whack," and the individual prominence in the discipline(s) [secured] by publications gives colleges and universities prominence in the world (Mathis and Holbrook 33).

> The over-arching effect of the differential reward system on the graduate student who seeks to develop his academic career goals is to diminish the clarity of his aspirations to gain teaching competence. (*Ibid.*51)

In 1975, FIPSE (Fund for the Improvement of Postsecondary Education) called for proposals to "elevate the importance of teaching." The Assembly on University Goals and Governance suggested that apprenticeship programs—with guidance and supervision provided by experienced teachers—be available for graduate students who intend to become professors (*American Higher Education: Toward an Uncertain Future* 332). But overall, graduate preparation programs, in general, and Ph.D. programs in particular, paid little attention to teacher training.

The quality of instruction at colleges and universities has been of special concern to many philanthropic foundations in the United States. Among the major foundations, the Kellogg Foundation provides "seed" money for activities that can later be carried on with internal funds, and the improvement of university teaching is one of their main objectives. The Danforth Foundation provided ten annual outstanding national teaching awards to individuals for a number of years and awarded fellowships to outstanding graduate students who were planning careers as college and university faculty members. The Carnegie Corporation is vitally concerned with the graduate degree structure and the appropriateness of the Ph.D. for college teaching. Since 1966 the Carnegie Corporation has generously seeded and funded the Doctor of Arts degree. The Ford Foundation provided increasing support to teaching improvement, much of it to minority colleges and universities to strengthen faculties and curricula. Innovation in undergraduate education, the external degree, and teacher preparation programs in colleges and universities are continuing foundation interests.

In the decades preceding World War II, research, although pre-eminent in the training of Ph.D's, produced less tangible income for institutions than did teaching (Berelson 40). Following World War II, faculty research grants brought added revenue to many institutions—especially for supplies, experimentation, and fringe efforts. General support for research, was, in the main, unrelated to teaching; and the rewards for research grew, while those for teaching remained stationary or diminished (Ben-David 107).

Still the Ph.D. continued to be considered the appropriate degree for college teachers. Historians marveled at the exceptional regard that existed for the Ph.D. in academic circles. According to the trends revealed in the literature, most Ph.D. recipients, in practice, become undergraduate teachers, and only a few remain exclusively in research. Somers in 1965 cited the experience of other nations, especially Britain, and suggested that "it is possible to prepare undergraduate college teachers without requiring the Ph.D." (530). And in the United States, too, there is no dearth of alternative degree proposals for the preparation of college teachers.

The Ph.D. degree has been criticized for almost a century as being inappropriate for college teaching and the associated responsibilities of student advisement and curriculum development (Eble 132; Dressel 167; Hecker 507). Stewart said that the Ph.D. system is designed to serve a few uniquely gifted people, but to keep abreast of an exploding undergraduate population "it has grown beyond its own source of nourishment" and has turned many graduates into cynics and time-servers. The Ph.D. "is no longer congruent with the needs of our society" (Stewart 786).

Alternative degree structures to better prepare college teachers have been frequently proposed, and sometimes adopted, in higher education. Such degree forms appear at various levels of graduate education. Master's, intermediate degrees, and doctorates compose the variety of American graduate teaching degrees.

A few Master of Philosophy and Master of Arts in Teaching

degrees were developed in the 1950s and 1960s to supply the need for lower-level college teachers. Despite attempts to strengthen the master's degree as an instrument to prepare college teachers, many educators felt that expanded master's degrees for college teaching would never be accepted because they were not doctorates. Few authors viewed this level degree to be totally acceptable for college teacher preparation (Cardozier 267; Volpe 775; Stewart 781).

Some educators wrote in the 1960s that the establishment of intermediate degrees might provide alternatives to the Ph.D. for students who wish to become college teachers on the undergraduate level. Also, the Association of Graduate Schools and the Council of Graduate Schools entertained discussions about intermediate degrees. Spurr listed intermediate degree designations in use then as *specialist, candidate, diplomate, scholar, director,* and *licentiate* (Spurr 98). The specialist degree, however, carried with it a professional "school of education" taint. Dunham termed this allegation the "kiss of death" to those seeking four-year college teaching positions (Dunham 511). Even though the title "specialist" is used among liberal arts disciplines, a stigma remains.

The Candidate in Philosophy certificate at the University of Michigan, the University of Minnesota, and the University of Washington represented a completed state in the Ph.D. program just short of the dissertation. Spurr explained that the Candidate in Philosophy is a "certificate" at all institutions except at the University of California, Berkeley, and the University of California, Los Angeles, where it is a "degree" (98). The Candidate in Philosophy certificate resembles Yale's Master of Philosophy degree in practice, declaring that all work toward the Ph.D. has been completed except the thesis. (Such a degree, however, may or may not include the college teaching component.)

The pressures for improvement of college and university teaching motivated several universities to strengthen or revise their Ph.D. programs. Societal and student pressures caused many graduate institutions to reduce, replace, or eliminate language requirements, and questions of residency in doctoral training continue to be debated. Nichols advocated three reforms for Ph.D. programs: (1) more effective programming of the Ph.D. curriculum, (2) at least a year of supervised training for all candidates seeking teaching positions, and (3) dissimilar track for pure research scholars (Nichols 334).

C. L. Barber at an Association of Departments of English meeting in 1965 felt a Ph.D. program "of quality" *could* prepare a student to be both teacher and scholar. Some departmental members felt a Ph.D. should only be awarded after two successful years of teaching experience—away from the degree-granting institution. Others felt teaching experience could eliminate the need of a dissertation for students who did not plan careers in research (Shulman).

The recent attempts to revise the Ph.D. degree resemble similar attempts in 1927. At that time the American Association of Universities found "the largest proportion of graduate students studying for the doctorate were intending to engage in college teaching and yet were receiving no specific training for that profession." Further, "A large number of young doctors of philosophy entering the college teaching field had been found ill-suited or inadequately prepared for the tasks of the profession" (Baxter 107). Having duly warned the graduate school members of these conditions, ten years later—in 1937—the A.A.U. surveyed the top forty-four graduate schools in the nation and found few outstanding or far-reaching changes had occurred since 1927 toward "professional preparation of Ph.D.'s for teaching." Baxter concluded that the situation regarding the preparation of Ph.D.'s for college teaching had regressed in ten years, rather than improved (117).

Heiss warned that initially only 50 percent of Ph.D.'s become college teachers, so adding a teaching component to Ph.D. programs can be wasted effort for the other half of the group. (Heiss 352). Is there, then, a great incentive for tailoring the Ph.D. to the needs of prospective college teachers? Harcleroad and others would reserve the Ph.D. for those planning research careers and provide special doctoral degrees for areas of applied knowledge (Shulman 5).

In 1961 Carmichael recommended that the college teaching

degree be a Doctor of Philosophy (*D. Phil.*) to distinguish it from a Ph.D., but graduate educators did not adopt the plan (Carmichael 201). Bowers felt a Doctor of Liberal Arts, requiring less time and giving much less emphasis to a dissertation, would be an adequate teaching doctorate. The D.L.A. would additionally protect the scholarly content of the Ph.D.; but the new degree idea was not popular.

In 1920 Harvard established the Doctor of Education (Ed.D) as a professional degree in their School of Education. At least one hundred institutions also awarded this degree, but for varying purposes. Spurr stated that the academic world feels the Ed.D. is a second-class degree, yet Columbia University, among others, has made a deliberate attempt to reinstate its quality. The Ed.D. is recommended as valid for a purely professional program, but very few educators consider it a *teaching* degree (Spurr 142).

The Doctor of Business Administration, Doctor of Social Sciences, Doctor of Social Work, Doctor of Architecture, and the Doctor of Nursing are popular, professionally oriented degrees identifying their fields. Indeed, many professional degree recipients teach in colleges and universities.

Heiss, in her survey of graduate faculty in prestigious universities, found 35 percent favored the introduction of a doctoral teaching degree in their fields (Heiss 285). Earlier, Keniston and Carmichael felt a new teaching doctorate would either be rejected or treated as a second-class degree (Keniston 44; Carmichael 122). Bigger, in 1966, built a case against the proliferation of doctorates, claiming that the employing institutional framework, rather than training, causes professors to neglect teaching. Heiss concluded:

> The arrangement against the heavy emphasis on research is that the majority of the Ph.D. holders who teach at the undergraduate or junior college level are over-prepared for activities they do not perform (research and publications) and unprepared for those they are obliged to perform (teaching, student advising, curriculum planning, evaluation, and test preparation). This affects

not only the quality of teaching at this level but creates problems of teaching morale. The flight from teaching is symptomatic of these facts. (356)

There is considerable resistance among community colleges to employ Ph.D.'s, even if they are in good supply, and many educators feel a research degree does not fit the needs of the community and junior colleges (Wallace 1974). The Carnegie Commission on Higher Education stated:

The historic degree structure has served America well. The dominant pattern for large segments of higher education is that already set in 1890—primary emphasis on the four-year B.A. and the six-and then eight- and then the ten-year Ph.D. as the degree of great prestige. This pattern of emphasis continues to meet the needs of many students, many campuses, and many occupations in 1970. The times, however, are changing. Relatively fewer students, fewer campuses, and fewer jobs are well served by the historic pattern. A fifth stage in the development of degree arrangements is now desirable. (*Carnegie Commission* 6)

The Assembly on University Goals and Governance further admonished:

Higher educational institutions in America, to their detriment, are imitative. The "front runners" are constantly aped by those with more limited resources. As a result, though, there are over 2,500 institutions, and they converge on a few models. Policies designed to produce greater differentiation, though difficult to fashion, are essential. Colleges and universities should become more discriminating in relating their resources to particular needs, less worried about their standing (often a mythical one) vis-a-vis other institutions, and more determined to develop experiments in every aspect of institutional life. If these things were done, the claim of

> American higher education to being pluralistic would
> begin to approach reality. (*American Higher Education:*
> *Toward an Uncertain Future* 344)

Optimal conditions in the late 1960s supported the idea of
a new doctoral teaching degree at some institutions. That
degree—the Doctor of Arts—promised to fill the critical void
existing in most Ph.D. programs—namely, the lack of teacher
training.

The Doctor of Philosophy degree has reigned supreme as
the ultimate academic credential in the USA for more than
a century. Its principal objective is to train students to publish
research results that are obtained through systematic inquiry.
However, in colleges and universities across the land the
overwhelming majority of faculty members who hold the Ph.D.
degree spend their working hours as college teachers. Yet very
few Ph.D. programs provide training for teaching.

Astute educators throughout the twentieth century
recognized the inconsistency between the *intended* and the
actual use made of the Ph.D. as a credential. As a remedy,
the Doctor or Arts degree was conceived and introduced in
the 1960s. It was launched with a good deal of seed money
supplied by The Carnegie Foundation at a number of
prestigious universities such as the University of Michigan,
Carnegie Mellon and the Catholic University.

The Doctor of Arts (DA) degree was carefully designed,
in content and form, and approved by the Council of Graduate
Schools in the U.S., the American Association of State Colleges
and Universities and the National Faculty Association of
Community and Junior Colleges. Generally, the DA program
includes these components: a major content area, one of more
cognate areas, a professional course component, a
comprehensive examination, research tool requirement(s), a
teaching internship, a project or dissertation, and a defense
of the culminating activity.

The Doctor or Arts degree emerged in response to a need
expressed for many decades—the need to train faculty to teach

as well as to do and interpret research. Whether the new degree form survives, and flourishes, depends on many factors. A century from now historians can judge whether the DA is or was a strong current in higher education or merely a ripple in the stream.

WORKS CITED

American Higher Education: Toward an Uncertain Future. Volume I. *Proceedings of the American Academy of Arts and Sciences.* Washington D.C., 1974.

Arrowsmith, William. "The Future of Teaching," in *Improving College Teaching.* C.B.T. Lee, ed. Washington: American Council on Education, 1967.

Barzun, Jacques. *Teacher in America.* Boston: Meador Press, 1945.

Baxter, E.J. "The Teaching Ph.D. Again." *Educational Record,* 20 (January, 1939), 107-117.

Ben-David, Joseph. *American Higher Education.* San Francisco: McGraw-Hill Book Co., 1972.

Berelson, B. *Graduate Education in the United States.* New York: McGraw-Hill Book Co., 1960.

Bigger, W.R. Innovations and Improvements in Graduate Study. *Proceedings of the Eighth Annual Meeting of the Western Association of Graduate Schools.* Los Angeles, CA, 1966.

Caffrey, John, ed. *The Future Academic Community.* Washington: American Council on Education, 1969.

Cardozier, V.R. "The Doctor of Arts Degree." *Journal of Higher Education,* 39 (May, 1968), 261-270.

Carmichael, O.C. *Graduate Education: A Critique and a Program.* New York: Harper and Brothers, 1961.

The Carnegie Commission on Higher Education. *Less Time, More Options.* New York: McGraw-Hill Book Co., 1971.

Council of Graduate Schools in the United States. "The Doctor of Arts Degree." Washington, DC, 1970.

Dressel, Paul L. *College and University Curriculum.* Berkeley, CA: McCutchen Publishing Co., 1971.

—————, and M. M. Thompson. *College Teaching: Improvement by Degrees.* Iowa City, IA: The American College Testing Program, 1974.

Dunham, E.A. "R for Higher Education: The Doctor of Arts Degree." *Journal of Higher Education,* 41 (October, 1970), 505-515.

Eble, Kenneth. *Professors as Teachers.* San Francisco: Jossey-Bass, Inc., 1972.

Flexner, Abraham. *Universities—American, English, German.* New York: Oxford University Press, 1930.

Hecker, Jo Anne K. "American Graduate Education: From Reverence to Relevance." *Intellect,* 104 (April, 1976), 505-507.

Heiss, Ann M. *Doctoral Education in Prestigious Universities.* Berkeley, CA: Center for Research and Development in Higher Education, University of California, 1970.

Hollis, E.V. *Toward Improving Ph.D. Programs.* Washington: American Council on Education, 1945.

Hyder, Clyde K. *George Lyman Kittredge. Teacher and Scholar.* Lawrence, Kansas: University of Kansas Press, 1962.

James, William. *Memories and Studies.* New York: Longmans, Green and Co., 1917.

Keniston, H.J. *Graduate Study and Research in the Arts and Sciences at the University of Pennsylvania.* Philadelphia: University of Pennsylvania, 1959.

Lehrer, Stanley, ed. *Leaders, Teachers, and Learners in Academe.* New York: Meredith Corporation, 1970.

Mathis, B.C. and S. T. Holbrook, ed. *Teaching: A Force for Change in Higher Education.* Evanston, Il: Northwestern University, The Center for the Teaching Professions, 1974.

McDonald, R. W., and J. L. McCaskill, ed. *Current Trends in Higher Education.* Washington: National Education Association of the United States, June, 1948.

Nichols, Roy F. "A Reconsideration of the Ph.D." *The Graduate Journal,* 7 (Spring, 1967), 325-335.

Rudolph, Frederick. *The American College and University.* New York: Vintage Books (Random House), 1962.

Shulman, Carol. "Preparing College Teachers." Compendium Series of Current Research, Programs, and Proposals. Washington: ERIC Clearinghouse on Higher Education, 1970. (ED 041 179)

Somers, Robert. "The Mainsprings of Rebellion: A Survey of Berkeley Students in 1964." *The Berkeley Student Revolt.* Edited by S. M. Lipset and S. Wolin. New York: Doubleday & Co., 1965.

Spurr, S.H. *Academic Degree Structure: Innovative Approaches.* New York: McGraw-Hill Book Co., 1970.

Stewart, D. H. "Prospects for the Doctor of Arts Degree." *College English,* 33 (April, 1972), 780-795.

Storr, R. J. *The Beginning of the Future*. New York: McGraw-Hill Book Co., 1973.

U.S. Commissioner of Education. *Report*. Washington: Government Printing Office, 1889-90.

Veysey, L. R. *The Emergence of the American University*. Chicago, Il: University of Chicago Press, 1965.

Volpe, E.L. "The Confessions of a Fallen Man: Ascent to the D.A." *College English*, 33 (April, 1972), 765-779.

Wallace, D.C. "A Functioning Program for the Preparation of Community College Biology Teachers." *American Biology Teacher*, 36 (1974), 99-101.

A Survey of the Status of the Doctor of Arts Degree in the United States

DA VID L. WHEELER
Dean, Graduate School and Research
Ball State University

The first doctor of arts degree was awarded by Carnegie-Mellon University in 1968. The degree was designed to prepare teacher-scholars for college training. Clark Kerr, Chairman of the Carnegie Commission on Higher Education said, "the Doctor of Arts should become the standard degree for college teaching in the United States."[1] Then, as now, skeptics saw the degree as a second class doctorate, low in quality and unmarketable. National surveys of the doctor of arts degree conducted at Ball State University since 1970 suggest that, while the degree has not become the standard for college teaching Kerr envisioned, neither has it been a failure.

Programs leading to the doctor of arts emphasize synthesis and dissemination of knowledge, not original research. Typical components of the degree are a broad subject matter specialization, a professional core of courses and seminars to prepare the candidate for college teaching, a structured teaching internship or, in some cases, an externship, and a dissertation. The dissertation does not necessarily contribute to new knowledge in a specialized field of study but, usually, it is related to the teaching of a subject and is considered applied in nature. These learning experiences are supervised, criticized, and evaluated by senior faculty members.[2]

By 1970, two years after Carnegie-Mellon conferred the first doctor of arts, there was ample evidence of interest in and support for the degree. The Committee on Graduate Studies of the American Association of State Colleges and Universities asserted there was a "definite need to provide another road to academic recognition and success, a road different from the Ph.D., particularly for those whose careers are in teaching.[3] The council of Graduate Schools in the United States endorsed, in principle, the establishment of doctor of arts programs and, in a statement a year later, outlined guidelines and standards.[4] The Carnegie Corporation of New York granted $935,000 to ten universities for program development and cooperated with the Johnson Foundation in sponsoring the first of two conferences on the doctor of arts.[5]

Between 1970 and 1988, eight national surveys were conducted by Ball State University on the status of the doctor of arts degree. Questionnaires were mailed to member institutions of the council of Graduate Schools in the United States and to a few non-member institutions offering doctoral programs. The number of questionnaires varied from 300 to 391 and returns were received from more than ninety percent of the institutions in each year but 1970 and 1988. The 1970 survey found three institutions offering the degree. By 1971, however, the number increased to sixteen in large measure a result of fund granting activity by the Carnegie Corporation the previous year. Twenty-six institutions were found to be offering the degree in the penultimate survey conducted in 1980.

The most recent survey on the status of the doctor of arts degree was conducted in May, 1988. A questionnaire was devised and sent to 392 institutions which included the member institutions of the Council of Graduate Schools in the United States and several others thought to be offering the doctor of arts degree. Nearly ninety percent of the institutions returned the questionnaire. The survey found that twenty-four institutions were offering the doctor of arts while one was planning to offer the degree and ten were considering the possibility.[6]

In 1988 there were thirty-eight different majors leading to the doctor of arts degree. Five institutions offered only one major but some offered several and the University of Miami (Florida) offered ten. The doctor of arts with a major in English was offered by nine institutions—four fewer than in the 1980 survey. The next most prevalent majors were chemistry with seven and mathematics with six. In at least four institutions, however, the degree in chemistry appears to be in trouble and in one institution, the University of Northern Colorado, it is being converted to a Ph.D. along with several other doctor of arts degree programs. After chemistry and mathematics, the next most prevalent majors are biology and history with five each, the latter down from seven in 1980. As in the case of one of the chemistry programs cited above, the doctor of arts degree program in biology and history are being converted to the Ph.D. at the University of Northern Colorado.

Several institutions are not admitting students to doctor of arts degree programs or have had no enrollments in recent years or, in the case of the University of Northern Colorado, are converting programs to the Ph.D. Ten institutions are considering the possibility of offering the doctor of arts degree. Only one institution plans to initiate a new major field of study leading to the degree.

In the spring term, 1988, 714 students were enrolled in doctor of arts degree programs at institutions responding to the survey. The largest number, 140, were enrolled in Nova University, followed by Illinois State University with 101, and George Mason University with eighty-six. The programs at Nova University and George Mason University have been established since the last survey in 1980. Three institutions reported no students enrolled. One institution did not know how many students were enrolled.

The survey found, also, that 700 doctor of arts degrees were awarded between 1979-80 and the end of the spring term 1988 or a total of 1509 degrees since the Ball State University survey was initiated in 1970. Forty-six degrees were awarded in 1970-1971, 117 in 1975-1976 the year of greatest productivity, and 102 in 1987-1988. If summer graduates were included in the 1987-1988 total, it is likely the total number of degrees awarded would have rivaled 1975-1976. In the 1980's, annual degree production has increased steadily from sixty-eight in 1980-1981 to 102 last year. The largest producers of doctor of arts degrees have been Middle Tennessee State University (ninety-five), the

University of Northern Colorado (ninety-three), and Idaho State University (eighty).

The survey sought to determine the employment found by doctor of arts graduates. Did the graduates find new positions, return to previous employment, or were they unemployed? Among the twelve institutions responding to questions on employment, it was found that fifty-four students or seventy-five percent of the total returned to previous employment, twelve or seventeen percent found new employment, and six or eight percent were not employed. Thus ninety-two percent of the doctor of arts recipients from twelve institutions were employed following graduation. Indeed, employment in an institution of higher education may be a condition of admission to a doctor of arts degree program.

The respondents were asked to identify the types of institutions or work settings in which their graduates were employed. The institutions or programs responding to this question could account for 401 graduates. Ninety-seven or twenty-four percent were employed in two-year or community colleges, 178 or forty-four percent were employed in four year colleges, and eighty-seven or twenty-seven percent were employed in public schools, most usually secondary schools, or in school administration.

Only one institution reported its doctor of arts degree recipients more difficult to place than graduates of other doctoral programs. Five reported doctor of arts recipients were more easily placed than other doctoral graduates and six reported there did not appear to be any difference in the placement of graduates holding various doctorates. Fourteen institutions had no opinion or did not report.

Despite the success doctor of arts degree recipients have had in finding employment, the degree has not gone without criticism. Each survey has contained space in the questionnaire to enable the respondent to comment on the degree. Respondents to the 1988 survey made fewer comments than in the past but these were similar to comments in previous surveys.

Concerns were expressed for the need, appeal, utility, and

credibility of the degree; its concept, standards, and quality. Some respondents stated the doctor of arts was "a degree whose time had come and gone." On the other hand, a number of respondents have found the doctor of arts an "excellent degree serving a critical need," its recipients "well-received and easily placed," and the degree a "valuable alternative" to other doctorates.

The influence of the doctor of arts degree cannot be assessed solely in terms of the output of the institutions offering the degree in 1988. An example of that influence is provided by the 1976 survey which found forty-three institutions offering doctoral programs similar to the doctor of arts and thirty-six institutions having sufficient flexibility in existing programs to offer a doctor of arts "type" degree. It is possible, of course, that since 1976 additional doctoral programs have been modified in response to the need for scholars who are capable teachers. If the doctor of arts degree has succeeded in no more than causing a reexamination of the goals of doctoral preparation, then it has made an important contribution to higher education.

NOTES

1. Carnegie Corporation of New York. News Release. 11 June 1970.

2. Robert H. Koenker, "The Doctor of Arts Degree," Conference on the Doctor of Arts Degree, New York University, 14 Nov. 1975. Also Paul L. Dressel and Mary M. Thompson, *A Degree for College Teachers: The Doctor of Arts* (Berkeley: Carnegie Council on Policy Studies in Higher Education, 1970) 12-13.

3. Committee on Graduate Studies of the American Association of State Colleges and Universities, *The Doctor of Arts Degree: A Proposal for Guidelines* (Washington, D.C.: AASCU, 1970).

4. The Council of Graduate Schools in the United States, *The Doctor of Arts Degree* (Washington, D.C.: CGS, 1970) 4. The Council of

Graduate Schools in the United States, *Supplemental Statement on the Doctor of Arts Degree* (Washington, D.C.: CGS, 1971).

5. See the Council of Graduate Schools in the United States, *Proceedings of the Wingspread Conference on the Doctor of Arts Degree* (Washington, D.C.: CGS, 1970) and the Council of Graduate Schools in the United States, *Analytical Models of Doctor of Arts Programs: Proceedings of the Second Wingspread Conference on the Doctor of Arts Degree* (Washington, D.C.: CGS, 1974). The conference participants were: Ball State University, Brown University, Claremont University Center, Dartmouth College, Idaho State University, Massachusetts Institute of Technology, State University of New York at Albany, the University of Michigan, the University of Washington, and Washington State University.

6. The twenty-four institutions offering the doctor of arts are: Adelphi University, Atlanta University, Ball State University, Catholic University of America, George Mason University, Idaho State University, Illinois State University, Lehigh University, Middle Tennessee State University, New York University, Nova University, Ohio State University, Simmons College, St. John's University (New York), State University of New York (Albany), State University of New York (Stonybrook), Syracuse University, University of Illinois (Chicago Circle), University of Miami (Florida), University of Michigan, University of Mississippi, University of Northern Colorado, University of North Dakota, and Washington State University. No students have enrolled in the doctor of arts degree programs at Ohio State University or Washington State University since 1976 and 1979 respectively.

A SURVEY OF THE STATUS
OF THE DOCTOR OF ARTS DEGREE IN THE
UNITED STATES, 1988

DAVID L. WHEELER
and
JACQUELYN S. NELSON
Ball State University

Question: Are you definitely planning on offering the Doctor of Arts degree at a future date? Are you currently considering the possibility of offering the D.A. degree in the future?

TABLE 1

NUMBER OF INSTITUTIONS OFFERING,
PLANNING TO OFFER,
OR CONSIDERING THE POSSIBILITY
OF OFFERING THE DOCTOR OF ARTS DEGREE

Year and Month of Study	Offer the D.A. Degree	Planning to Offer D.A. Degree	Considering the Possibility of Offering D.A. Degree
November, 1970	3	27	46
November, 1971	16	11	60
November, 1972	20	7	33
January, 1974	22	3	23
January, 1975	23	6	20
February, 1976	24	4	33
May, 1980	26	2	9
July, 1988	24	1	10

TABLE 2
INSTITUTIONS OFFERING THE DOCTOR OF ARTS

Adelphi University	St. John's University
Atlanta University	Simmons College
Ball State University	State University of New York-Albany
Catholic University of America	State University of New York-Stonybrook
George Mason University	Syracuse University

Idaho State University	University of Illinois-Chicago Circle
Illinois State University	University of Miami-Coral Gables
Lehigh University	University of Michigan
Middle Tennessee State University	University of Mississippi
New York University	University of North Dakota
Nova University	University of Northern Colorado
Ohio State University	Washington State University

Question: Name your major field(s) of study for the Doctor of Arts Degree and the year the major was instituted.

TABLE 3

DOCTOR OF ARTS MAJORS OFFERED BY TWENTY-FOUR INSTITUTIONS

Major	No. of Institutions Offering Major	Major	No. of Institutions Offering Major
Art Education	1	Information Science	1
Art Therapy	1	Information Systems	1
Biology	5	Inter-American Studies	1
Civil Engineering	1	International Affairs	1
Chemistry	7	Library & Information Center	
Community College Teaching	1	Management	1
Creative Arts	1	Mathematics	6
Dance Education	1	Mechanical Engineering	1
Dance Performance	1	Modern Language (Spanish)	1
Dance Therapy	1	Modern World History	1
Economics	3	Music***	3
Education	1	Music Education	1
English*	9	Music Performance	1
English Language and		Music Therapy	1
Literature	1	Physical Education	1
Foreign Languages	3	Political Science****	2
Geography	1	Physics	1
Government**	1	Speech Pathology & Audiology	1
History	4	Studio Art	1
Humanities	2	Training and Learning	1

  *One program no longer admitting students
  **Being phased out
  ***One program being replaced by Ph.D.
  ****One program eliminated in 1983

Question: Are you planning to add any new majors? If yes,
please name the major field of study and the year
the program will be initiated.

TABLE 4

PLAN OF ONE INSTITUTION TO ADD
D.A. DEGREE MAJOR

Institution	New Major	Predicted Date to be Added
A	Physical Sciences	1991

Question: If available, please report the number of D.A.
degrees awarded per year 1979-1980 through the
end of the spring term, 1988.

TABLE 5

NUMBER OF DOCTOR OF ARTS
DEGREES AWARDED BY TWENTY-ONE
INSTITUTIONS 1979-1988

Inst.	79-80	80-81	81-82	82-83	83-84	84-85	85-86	86-87	87-88	Total
A	0	0	0	0	0	0	0	5	0	5
B	0	0	0	1	0	0	1	5	8	15
C	11	10	7	8	7	12	7	5	14	81
D	2	2	3	3	5	1	2	1	0	19
E	8	7	6	10	17	17	11	6	13	95
F	0	0	0	0	0	0	2	10	13	25
G	0	0	0	1	2	0	2	2	2	9
H	3	2	3	2	2	3	2	3	2	22
I	4	2	9	7	5	9	13	7	12	68
J	0	1	1	3	5	2	1	2	4	19
K	1	0	1	1	0	0	1	1	2	7
L	6	3	5	9	6	1	4	2	4	40
M	2	6	3	1	1	2	1	2	0	18
N	6	3	2	0	2	0	1	5	1	20
O	7	12	16	12	13	13	9	7	4	93
P	1	0	0	0	0	0	0	0	0	1
Q	1	0	0	1	1	3	2	5	1	14

R	4	14	5	4	5	4	8	9	5	58
S	7	2	7	5	2	8	6	8	14	59
T	3	3	2	2	2	3	1	0	0	16
U	1	1	2	1	3	4	0	1	3	16
Totals	67	68	72	71	78	82	74	86	102	700

Question: How many of your spring term D.A. degree graduates have obtained *new* positions on graduation? How many of your spring term D.A. degree graduates have returned to present positions on graduation? How many spring term D.A. degree graduates were not placed on graduation?

TABLE 6

EMPLOYMENT OF D.A. GRADUATES FOR TWELVE INSTITUTIONS

Institution	Number of Graduates Placed in New Positions	Number of Graduates Returning to Previous Position	Not Placed	Total
A	0	1	0	1
B	1	14	0	15
C	4	1	0	5
D	0	8	2	10
E	0*	13	0	13
F	0	0	1	1
G	1	1	0	2
H	3	4	2	9
I	1	3	0	4
J	0	1	0	1
K	0	2	0	2
L	2	6	1	9
Totals	12	54	6	72

*Prerequisite to be employed in the field

Question: Name your major field(s) of study for the Doctor of Arts Degree and the year the major was instituted.

TABLE 7

YEAR D.A. MAJOR(S) INSTITUTED AMONG TWENTY INSTITUTIONS

Year	Number of Majors Instituted
1970	13
1971	6
1972	2
1973	16
1974	3
1975	3
1976	2
1977	9
1979	1
1980	4
1983	1
1984	1
1985	1
1986	1
1987	1
1988	1

Question: If your institution offers other doctoral programs, e.g., Ph.D., Ed.D., etc., what are they?

TABLE 8

OTHER TYPES OF DOCTORATES OFFERED BY TWENTY-ONE D.A. DEGREE GRANTING INSTITUTIONS

Combination of Doctorates Offered	Number of Institutions Offering This Combination
Ph.D., Ed.D., D.A.	10
Ph.D., J.D., D.A.	1

Ph.D., D.A.	3
D.W.S. and D.A.	1
Ph.D., Ed.D., D.P.A., Psy.D., D.A.	1
Ph.D., D.M.A., D.A.	1
Ph.D., Ed.D., D.M.A., M.D., J.D., D.A.	1
Ph.D., Ed.D., Psy.D., D.M.E., D.A.	1
Ph.D., Ed.D., Psy.D., D.A.	1
D.A. only doctorate offered	1

Question: Please feel free to make any comments you wish regarding the Doctor of Arts degree.

COMMENTS
BY SCHOOLS HAVING D.A. DEGREE

D.A. had more appeal in the early 1970's than now. Preference today is for the Ph.D.

Graduates are well received and easily placed if not particular about geographic location. This degree works well and meets the expectations of the new emphasis on teaching.

With the exception of music, the D.A. still suffers from a credibility problem.

D.A.'s are difficult to place.

An appropriate substitute for the Ph.D. or Ed.D., not *less*, but different.

COMMENTS BY SCHOOLS
NOT OFFERING D.A. DEGREE

No rational standard for or agreement upon amount of academic work in D.A. programs.

D.A. serves no useful purpose and is ill conceived.

D.A. is outside the mainstream of academia.

Valuable alternative for states with need.

Too many poorly defined degrees already exist.

Excellent degree serving a critical need.

D.A. degree is a concept that has come and gone.

As long as there are unplaced Ph.D.'s, D.A.'s will be unemployable.

D.A. is a "consolation prize," a "second-line" degree.

Equivalent doctorates are already available.

Does the D.A. Have a Future?

MARTIN KANES

Director, D.A. Program in Humanistic Studies

SUNY/Albany

Academics and stockholders traditionally gather either to congratulate themselves or to prevent the sky from falling down. I guess we are here today to do a bit of both. On the one hand, the D.A. degree is currently awarded by some twenty universities around the country (meriting congratulations all round); on the other hand its holders are having a difficult time competing with those in possession of a Ph.D. (making us feel as if we have to shore up the sky). Let me suggest that if we do not merit quite the back-patting we like to award ourselves, neither do we have to put a prop under the heavens. As always, the truth is somewhere in between. Let me further suggest that these successes and failures are linked to the structure of the D.A.—that is, to the relationship it establishes, or fails to establish, between teaching and research. And so we have before us the two issues with which this panel is concerned: the structure of the degree, and its marketability. Let me sketch some background and then deal with the two topics in the order in which I mentioned them.

The Doctor of Arts degree was created partly as a response to a perceived conflict between teaching and research. It was proposed to train specialists in higher education whose chief focus would be on the former rather than the latter. This was a reaction to the widely-held view that the traditional Ph.D. placed undue emphasis on research; a view which, in its turn, was based on the assumption that research and teaching competed with each other for a professor's time and energy. Although in a strict sense this is true (one can't be doing two things at the same time) the argument seems to me to be flawed for two reasons:

1. First and most important, such a view is narrowly

quantitative. I still recall the parting message given me by my graduate school mentor: "Remember," he said, "the only thing that counts is the number of pages per year." It was probably the worst advice I ever got, but I do not blame the giver: he was merely reflecting the assumptions of his times. You may or may not have quality, but you surely have to have quantity, even if that quantity is achieved at the expense of teaching. This was the old "publish or perish" principle, of course. Even at its best, it wasn't always effective. You may recall a cartoon on the subject, showing two academics looking at a memorial plaque to a departed colleague. "Poor Turnbull," one is saying, "he published but he still perished." We all know Turnbulls—some of them untenured and as yet undeparted. In a word there is something phoney about the way we regard research.

2. Second, we tend to ignore the fact that the connection between teaching and research varies radically from field to field, and from one level of instruction to another. Let us assume that we are talking about real research, not the publishing mill. Undergraduate education in the sciences, for example, has very little to do with work being done in the research laboratory, whereas *graduate* education in the sciences has everything to do with the research laboratory. In the humanities, on the other hand, it is common for creative ideas to emerge from teaching at any level, and conversely to affect teaching at all levels. To say, therefore, that a degree places stress on teaching as distinct from research means different things in different fields.

But our society is technological, and natural science sets the model for higher education. As natural scientists move further and further down the dark hallways of their fields, they find fewer and fewer colleagues and students with whom to speak. Teaching truly becomes an impediment, a distraction, except for dialogue with the advanced graduate students who are supported by grants and who will eventually become the fourth, fifth or sixth "authors" of the articles that emerge from the project. Of what use to such a person is a Doctor of Arts degree? Only a diploma heavily stressing research, and only from specific institutions and indeed from specific laboratories within those institutions, will do. In a word, it seems to me that in the natural sciences, except only at the very highest level, the teaching-research relationship is indeed adversarial.

The creators of the D.A. responded by saying, "Very well, let the technologist and science researchers do their thing, and let Ph.D.'s in the humanities imitate them; *we* will be professional teachers." But what did this actually turn out to mean? All too often it meant merely the combination of disciplinary courses (most frequently English or History) with education courses: in a word, a variation to the D. Ed. At the same time, collegiate institutions wanted "researchers" in the classic sense of the term, and not just in the sciences. The last thing they wanted was a degree that seemed, fairly or unfairly, "tainted" with educationalism.

So the D.A. was fraught with problems from the moment it was born. Created to separate out "teaching" from "research" it appeared to misconstrue what "teaching" meant and it flew in the face of the fact that the connection is in any case discipline-bound. But having accepted the premise of the Ph.D. structure, the D.A. was inevitably left, sociologically speaking, with the short end of the stick. Why, then, are we surprised that the degree has not "caught on" better than it has? In my own view, the only chance for a viable Doctor of Arts degree would have been to have reaffirmed the inextricable intertwining of teaching and creative research in the humanities and social sciences and to have found a more attractive way to link them.

Clearly a small group interested in promoting a degree cannot reverse such powerful cultural trends as we face today. At SUNY-Albany we recognized the facts of life. We created two D.A. degrees, one in English and one in Humanistic Studies, and sought to configure them in such a way that they did not compete with the Ph.D. They were simply designed to do different things. I don't mean to claim that we were particularly prescient or gifted. In part we were forced to find alternatives because of a 1960's anti-Ph.D. hysteria in the State of New York; in part we just fell into a pattern that served us well. We are a relatively young institution (founded in 1848 as a Normal School, transformed into a general campus in 1965), and thus perhaps less bound to tradition than most institutions. Without boasting, let me say that statistics have tended to validate our assumptions. Now in its fifth year of operation, the D.A. in Humanistic Studies has graduated its first two D.A.'s and has about 35 enrolled students; at the beginning of its 17th year of operation, the D.A. in English has graduated 75 degree-holders and has about 75 currently enrolled students, of which approximately 40 constitute the active "core."

Let me describe our situation briefly because it explains in part the nature of our programs, and may also contain elements of general usefulness.

SUNY-Albany is located in the capital district of the State of New York, and is thus surrounded by—overwhelmed by— state agencies, bank headquarters, corporate headquarters, and the various administrative accumulations that one would expect. This means that we have a potential local clientele of considerable size, and one with non-academic career interests. Furthermore, the state possesses many private post-secondary institutions in all degrees of quality and size. We recognize a marginal market here, for both English and Humanistic Studies.

The campus is part of the system of the State University of New York as well, which includes not only the four University Centers (Albany, Binghamton, Buffalo and Stony Brook) but also fifty-nine other units ranging from four-year colleges down (if I may use that figure of speech) to community colleges and technical schools. This area, too, could be expected to yield a potential clientele of a particular academic nature.

Finally, on the national scene the campus is now emerging as one of the top 100 universities in the country in terms of grant dollars received, if despite all, I may use that yard-stick; but more importantly it has been steadily building a faculty of national and indeed international stature in many fields.

In this context we were faced, in the 1960's and 1970's, with the task of creating and maintaining viable doctoral-level programs. We had many disciplinary Ph.D. programs, of course. But the "zap" work in those days was "innovative"; the State of New York was not interested in proliferating Ph.D.'s, especially in view of those somber predictions that used to be made by demographers about how we were going to have practically no students in the 1980's and 1990's. We had to look for different angles, and this is what we came up with:

Rather than require a set of education courses or "how to" seminars, our D.A. in English provides all graduate students with an elaborate training procedure specifically designed to develop professionalism. Insofar as prospective teachers are concerned, that means the very careful training of students in *all* the activities one would expect of an academic: problem-specific classroom techniques (the teaching of writing being quite different, say, from the teaching of the novel), research methodology, the preparation and presentation of professional papers, and so on. In a word the English faculty tries to encourage the integration of research and teaching in the most mutually-enriching ways possible. It actually tries to develop the skills to which many Ph.D. programs pay only lip service. That is one way in which it really is different from a Ph.D. Additionally, the degree somewhat de-emphasizes traditional literary history and criticism in favor of certain special areas in which the faculty has nationally recognized strengths: rhetoric, discourse analysis, and creative writing. Ultimately, the degree is meant to be appropriate not only for prospective teachers, but also for writers, editors and individuals specializing in other areas of writing. Consequently, all students are required to do *some* work in critical theory and practice, language and language theory, and writing theory and practice. These arrangements have brought us some success, although in the placement of academically-oriented students the competition with the Ph.D. in English still crops up. Graduates with non-academic interests are now placed in a variety of positions in journalism, publishing, and so forth.

Let me concentrate now on the D.A. in Humanistic Studies, because I direct the program and know it intimately. In designing it, we deliberately moved away from the Ph.D.

"teaching and research" model and indeed away from the "large university faculty" career model. In fact, we decided to go after an entirely different clientele, one that did not necessarily plan on careers in teaching. This entailed a different attitude toward research. We could do this partly because of the specific location of SUNY-Albany in a state capital, as I have mentioned; and it may be one of the lessons of our experience that the D.A. cannot thrive in just any atmosphere.

The Clientele we had in mind was the following:

1. Those wishing to teach in high schools, two-year campuses, or four-year colleges without graduate programs.

2. Those having non-academic career plans in government, foundations, libraries, archives and certain parts of the private sector.

3. It did *not* include those wishing to become faculty members at large, research institutions, or at four-year colleges having Master's programs.

In a word, we did not try to beat the Ph.D. at its own game.

We seek our students in a large and sophisticated local and national clientele through an extensive mailing program. We will not accept any student whose study plan goes beyond the facilities available at the University, or whose program does not make intellectual sense, or whose career plans cannot reasonably be expected to be furthered by this degree. The consequence is that our student body is extraordinarily pragmatic in outlook. It is also extraordinarily diverse. We have freshly minted B.A.'s, government employees, secondary school teachers and administrators, and two- and four- year college faculty. And because of our University's active exchange arrangements with foreign institutions, we have students from England, France, Spain, Brazil, China, and Ghana.

Having delineated our clientele, we then sought to structure the degree in a way that would immediately distinguish it from the Ph.D. We made it interdisciplinary and generalist by definition; not the way in which interdisciplinary Ph.D.'s are usually constructed (a disciplinary Ph.D with some extra trimmings thrown in), but truly so. And indeed, its interdisciplinary nature has proven to be one of its most attractive qualities. We sometimes have to advise students that because of their interests they really ought to be in Ph.D. programs; but just as often we receive refugees from Ph.D. programs who heave huge sighs of relief at being released from what they regard as the restrictions of a specialist education. (It should also be mentioned that the word "interdisciplinary" for some reason tends to attract a certain proportion of "kooky" applicants: I haven't figured out why).

The shape of the program, then, is the following:

1. It requires work in two fields, one of which must be in the humanities (the other may be humanistic, social scientific, or even professional—for example librarianship or arts administration)

2. It has a small (really small: only three courses) core of specially designed, required, interdisciplinary, team-taught courses that bind the whole thing together.

3. It requires an internship, a qualifying examination, and a dissertation project that can take an appropriately non-traditional form.

Beyond the three required core courses, no two students follow precisely the same program. They must satisfy certain "category" requirements, but how they do so depends on their study plan.

One problem with which we wrestled extensively was how to avoid creating a kind of intellectual buffet, a sampling of this and that leading to no unified concept. We concluded that we would organize the program around the notion that symbols and symbols systems were the characteristics that defined human nature and consciousness; if you will, a kind of humanistic semiotics. This approach is incorporated into our group core Colloquia. There might have been other unifying concepts—and we are currently looking into alternatives—but that was the one we chose.

There is, though, another level of linkage essential to any such program. That is the two-way binding element that holds together individual student programs. As you can imagine, the number of combinations of fields is limited only by the resources of the campus; but not all combinations make sense. This being the case, we have a two-stage admissions procedure. As a first step, all applicants must submit a program Proposal in which they identify the two fields that interest them as well as the link connecting them. One could, for example, propose the fields of English Literature and History, and as the link cite the analysis of literature as historical evidence, and of historiography as a kind of creative writing. The two-way relationship thus established could even eventually lead to a certain conception of a dissertation topic. Students who find this first step to be one of the most difficult in the whole program. It requires them to think through what they want to do with graduate work (rather than merely "do" it); it also forces them to articulate the sorts of intellectual problems that attract them.

There are difficulties, of course. One of them is endemic to interdisciplinary programs: how to provide students with sufficient expertise in *two* fields without making the course of study too long and arduous. We are careful to tell students that we are not training them to "be" philosophers or historians or literary critics. We aim to create generalists and to give them enough tools in their two fields so that they can apply the techniques and insights of each on the other. We try to assure this adequacy through careful selection of courses, a qualifying examination based upon reading lists jointly developed by student and faculty, and by closely supervised internships.

Students have responded with enthusiasm. The kind of research they do is not "simpler" than that of Ph.D. students; it is just different. For those who do indeed wish to teach, research is closely linked to their teaching activities via the internship. One dissertation combined theater and education in an analysis of the American Musical as a teaching device; another now being written deals with the philosophical bases of anthropology. For non-teaching students, the links vary widely. We have dissertations under way dealing with urbanization and quality of life in Ghana, on the structure of Proto-Thai and its relationship to southeast asian culture, and so on. Other students are planning dissertation projects linking such fields as English and Arts Administration, where research has to do with the way in which regional theaters pick, produce, and market their programs. The range of topics, as you can see, is enormous. One of my most striking experiences occurred a few weeks ago, when a Ghanaian student was presenting his Dissertation Proposal to a Round Table of fellow students for comment and critiquing (this is a requirement of the program). He was closely questioned by a student from mainline China as to the interdisciplinary aspects of his work. There were two of them, from opposite ends of the earth, sitting in Albany discussing the nature of interdisciplinarity in a language foreign to them both. It was a remarkable discussion and a memorable evening, and it convinced me that these students will make their marks in their own ways.

A successful program requires more than an appropriate structure and good students. It simply cannot exist without the involvement of faculty who truly believe in its viability. We accomplish this in a variety of ways. Each student's activities are supervised by a panel of at least three professors drawn from appropriate fields; there are now about fifty such faculty panel members. The humanities committee itself, which is responsible for administering the program, includes individuals drawn from diverse departments and schools of the university. Perhaps most important, our students attend graduate seminars along with Ph.D. students in the various disciplines; they get to be known by the faculty who are thereby encouraged to become involved in the program.

Additionally, the Core colloquia are not partially team-taught, and as of next year will all be team-taught. This has been a hugely successful experience for all of us. As of this next semester, we are adding an interesting wrinkle: we are going to have regular Monday late-afternoon sherry hours at which the team members will discuss the topics and issues dealt with in the core colloquia. Our first bottle of Dry Sack has already been spoken for.

What of the future? I think that the anticipated shortage

of university faculty will give renewed impetus to the restoration and institution of Ph.D. programs. And I think it is delusion to hope that the D.A. will be able to compete with the Ph.D. for those kinds of jobs. The future of the D.A. lies in the careful and precise definition of its range and purpose: in our case it was teaching and administration up to but not including the research university; careers in government, foundations, libraries, archives, publishing houses and other such institutions; public service organizations both cultural (theaters, orchestras, etc.) and charitable; and last but surely not least, personal development, which we have found to be a very strong motivation indeed among our older students. That already seems like a great deal. Whatever our students achieve beyond that will depend upon their personal talents—as it always does. Correctly seen, then, the future seems to me to be quite bright. The D.A. is not for every institution and not for every student, and surely not for every purpose. But there are very many students out there who want something other than the old model, and if we play our cards right we can attract them.

Evolution and Change in Graduate Education: the Doctor of Arts in English at the University of Michigan

RICHARD W. BAILEY
Director, D.A. Programs
University of Michigan/Ann Arbor

Twenty years after my colleagues and I began to give serious thought to a new doctoral degree in English, I welcome the opportunity to review what we eventually accomplished.[1] Or, better said: to celebrate what the students who had the courage to risk their careers in our optimism have achieved in their graduate study and beyond.

Most people are familiar with *Hawthorne effect*, a term that arose from the time-and-motion studies carried out at a Western Electric plant in Cicero, Illinois, in the 1930s. Here is what the *Random House Dictionary of the English Language* (second edition) offers by way of definition:

> *Hawthorne effect.* a positive change in the performance of a group of persons taking part in an experiment or study due to their perception of being singled out for special consideration.

In the study at the Hawthorne plant, the experimenters found that women assembling relays increased their productivity when lighting was increased *and* when lighting remained the same *and* when lighting was decreased. By being "singled out" for special treatment, whatever the lighting conditions, they did their jobs better.

Some of the success for faculty and students involved in the Doctor of Arts program is surely to be attributed to the

Hawthorne Effect, a result of the idea in which we believed
and which the students came to believe—that we were engaged
in a new, experimental initiative in graduate study in English.
(When people cite the Hawthorne effect, they usually neglect
the companion study in the same plant in which men engaged
in a collective enterprise of constructing relay boards were found
to exert social pressure to hold down productivity. That part
of the Hawthorne effect needs to be considered too—the
tendency of people in an organization to band together to
protect their jobs and to maintain the status quo of the
workplace culture.) Oblivious to the problems we faced, we
set out to persuade the Graduate School to institute the degree.

This enterprise was funded, in its initial stages, by the
Carnegie Corporation which responded to the then popular
notion that Ph.D. holders were likely to be good scholars but
not necessarily first-rate teachers. Earlier in the 1960s, the Ford
Foundation had provided funds to ensure that the students
on the way to the Ph.D. would gain teaching experience and
even some training in how to do it. With the results of that
effort still invisible, Carnegie then decided that major
universities should be challenged to institute a new degree that
would have the effect of improving undergraduate teaching.
In this initiative, Carnegie was strongly supported by the
Council of Graduate Schools which envisioned a terminal
degree for teaching equal in rigor and prestige to the Ph.D.

Some of the Carnegie money supported planning activities,
and, before the students who formed the first D.A. cohort
were admitted in 1971, we used those welcome funds to visit
the kinds of institutions where we expected D.A. students to
teach English: community colleges (especially those in urban
areas) and vocational-technical institutes. Representatives from
those places became our advisors in telling us what kind of
education they thought best suited their needs. Without
compensation (beyond their travel expenses), they came to Ann
Arbor to help us design the program. Of the many they offered,
these three points sum up the ideas (then and now) behind
the degree: recruit highly-motivated and experienced teachers;
let them have the greatest latitude in drawing upon the resources

of the University; help them to return to the classroom not only with a credential but also with an increased appetite for innovative teaching. The advisors also endorsed the idea that students on the way to degrees should have extra time for a teaching internship in which to test ideas they had developed during their study in Ann Arbor; this excellent suggestion resulted in degree holders who had become "teacher-researchers" (though that fashionable term had yet to be invented).

For the new degree title to be accepted, however, we were obliged to present our proposal to the Executive Board of the Graduate School and subsequently to a hearing before a well-attended meeting of the graduate faculty. Many supported the idea, and we had especially welcome allies in our School of Music where faculty were supportive of a degree designed with practitioners in mind.[2] One opponent was Professor Darwin Turner (then at Michigan) who regarded the D.A. proposal as a racially motivated effort to divert minorities from the Ph.D. program into something less rigorous and less prestigious. Certainly we who proposed the degree had no such intention, but whether they were diverted or attracted, our D.A. program has been especially hospitable to minorities. (Many, but by no means all, sought and found opportunities to study and write about minority literature and related topics.) Turner called for something more radical— a reconsideration of the Ph.D. requirements in light of what people who receive that degree do when they have finished. We believed that we could accomplish more by adding something new rather than challenging directly the tradition that doctoral study recruits only people in their early twenties, requires at least five years beyond the bachelor's degree, and can only be pursued after various kinds of study quite unrelated to one's future career.

Hindsight persuades us that our objectives were in response to a long history in colleges and universities of seeking "qualified" people and, for some groups at least, seldom finding any. In our first group and since, we have recruited doctoral candidates with twenty and more years of teaching, minorities in proportions approximating their representation in the general population, and women returning to teaching jobs once their children are in school or have reached adulthood. But that's a view informed by hindsight; what we first did was to recruit people who were excellent teachers seeking advanced study that would enrich their teaching. The rest followed. This openness to greater variety in the graduate student cohort is now much more common, partly by force of law and partly by the inclinations of a younger generation of faculty serving now on admissions committees. but in 1969-70 when we were young faculty, we decided to try out the assumption that people were successful until they and we were persuaded otherwise. It was a novel idea in those days; it is an idea regarded with suspicion even now.

The accompanying table shows subjects investigated in completed D.A. dissertations at Michigan. Just more than half of the degrees awarded have composition as their focus—two thirds if we include technical communication and basic literary pedagogy in that category. Such an outcome was the natural result of our program definition: to help experienced teachers continue careers in teaching typical of the first two years of undergraduate study. But what is also of interest is the number of students concentrating in fields now much in demand by university English departments: topics involving minorities and minority literature, topics arising from studies of professional-technical writing, topics exploring issues of feminism (a number that would be larger were it not for the abrupt acknowledgement of topics concerning women in longer-established doctoral programs). Many of these subjects were not encouraged by the other doctoral programs at Michigan, and, though rare students did complete the Ph.D. with a focus on composition or minority literature, they did so despite the advisors who thought "unconventional" topics would have career-impairing consequences.

Dissertation Topics
Doctor of Arts in English
The University of Michigan

		1973 - 77	1978 - 82	1983 - Present
Composition		28	19	11
Literary Topics		3	2	2
Minorities	Arabs	-	-	2
	Blacks	5	2	4
	Gays	-	1	1
	Hispanics	-	1	-
	Native Americans	-	1	3
Popular Culture		6	-	-
Technical Communication		-	1	2
Women's Issues		1	1	1
Other		6	1	1
	TOTALS	49	29	27

Two shifts in the numbers found in this table are of interest. The first is the disappearance of dissertations devoted to popular culture. When we began, we encouraged students to seek links between what undergraduates knew and what we wanted them to learn—for instance, the connection between lyrics in rock-and-roll songs and lyrics enshrined in the literary canon. With the death of Marvin Felhiem, who had been a compelling and imaginative teacher of popular culture, this emphasis diminished. A second shift in the numbers shows a decline from 49 degrees completed in the first five years to 29 and 27 in the second and third five-year periods. That change calls for more extended discussion.

With the Hawthorne effect illuminating our work during those first years of the program, we admitted and taught more students than later. Partly the decline can be traced to the phasing out of our external funding designated for D.A. financial aid.[3] But the more interesting reason arises from other initiatives attracting the attention of the core faculty. Many of us worked to develop writing assessments, inaugurate writing-across-the-curriculum, and staff cooperative ventures in teaching involving schools in the region. By the late 70s, the D.A. program was no longer a fresh new venture, and, if it had not yet become routine, it had become a familiar part of our teaching and a reflection of our research interests. Several of these faculty became so caught up in these new ideas that they drifted away from the old new idea that had proved to be such a success. None of us had been recruited to Michigan in the expectation that we would found a D.A. program (or anything remotely similar). But we were persuaded to try something new in the bright optimism of the late 1960s. Now, in these gloomier times, and even though the D.A. program has proved its worth to those who have earned the degree and its value to the prestige of the University of Michigan, no faculty have been hired with the idea that they would teach in the D.A. program. Our innovation became institutionalized and continues to occupy the engaged attention of some of the core faculty. But, like D.A. programs elsewhere, it now needs the commitment of a second and third generation of innovators, whether specifically recruited for that role or attracted from within the department.

"Just Say No" is a campaign made popular in Washington recently. But American universities have long practiced that preachment when confronted with new ideas for graduate education. Newly established Ph.D. programs in English, drawing on NDEA support from the federal government in the late 1950s and early 1960s, usually rivalled or surpassed the longer-established programs in the "rigor" and number of their requirements (ensuring that graduates would not be found ignorant of any area ever included in any English curriculum). The climate of the workplace, then and now, favors faculty who refuse admission to students (whose success or lack thereof can never then be measured against the criteria applied in rejecting them); similarly, those who vote against retaining younger colleagues working in "unconventional" fields enjoy the esteem of their "tough-minded" peers and rarely suffer any consequence of a bad decision. This climate of belief, cautious and conservative, has had (and continues to have) unfortunate consequences for D.A. students and degree holders.

D.A. students at Michigan have, from the beginning, accumulated higher grade point averages than other graduate students. Yet it is still a commonplace for some faculty to wonder why this or that year's bright student is in the D.A. program rather than on the Ph.D track. Their wonder is even greater if they discover that D.A. students have chosen the D.A. even though admitted to (or admissible to) the Ph.D. In this climate of belief, D.A. students do not often succeed in competition for academic prizes—except for teaching awards where they enjoy exceptional success—partly because their subjects are often outside the channel of a professional mainstream so roughly managed that the Army Corps of Engineers would look favorably on its angularity. On the job market, D.A. students may have to explain that, at Michigan at least, they take more and more varied course work than other doctoral students and that they complete dissertations equal in scholarship to those of others. Once employed, they may have to meet higher expectations, and more than once I have been obliged to write to a dean or other executive officer considering promotion cases to explain just what sort of degree the D.A. is.[4]

But that is the bad news. The good news is that the fine teachers we recruited for the D.A. have become leaders in the profession. Many of them appear annually on the program of the conference on College Composition and Communication. They often manage introductory composition programs or writing centers. They speak at professional meetings and publish books and scholarly articles about as often as graduates of our Ph.D. program. They set the agenda in the fields of their specialization.

It would be tempting to close by taking credit for all of these achievements. But the success of the D.A. at Michigan arises from the students rather than from their teachers. They are unusual people. Far more than recent bachelor's-degree graduates, they are committed to their careers. They make a financial sacrifice to take time out for graduate study. They achieve the doctoral degree even though they recognize that, in many community colleges, the credential does not translate automatically into a salary increase. Our D.A. students select themselves. Without further graduate study or with a different doctoral degree, many would have been influential in their classrooms and beyond. But the D.A. program has brought together people who have learned from each other, valued cross-disciplinary work with uncommon enthusiasm, collaborated in research and publication, and formed life-long friendships. We continue to believe that all we need to do is to provide opportunities. They accomplish the rest.

What is the future of the Doctor of Arts degree? Nationally, it will continue to be offered at institutions where it is the only doctoral degree awarded. At Michigan, it will continue as an alternative to the Ph.D., as our quick-response degree— one so little burdened with specific course requirements that motivated and experienced teachers can use the opportunities it provides to study areas of new interest. Their dissertations and subsequent contributions to the profession will, I am confident, be as important as those of the graduates who have established its reputation in the first fifteen years.

NOTES

1. I want here to name those who began our D.A. program or who subsequently took major administrative responsibility for it: William R. Alexander, Walter Clark, Timothy G. Davies, Daniel N. Fader, Marvin Felheim, Alan B. Howes, Jay L. Robinson, and Bernard van't Hul.

2. Since the 1950s, the School of Music has offered a performance doctorate, the Doctor of Musical Arts. At a recent symposium on graduate education at Michigan, Dean Paul Boylan recalled how eastern music critics scorned the idea of a doctoral degree combining,

for instance, musicology, theory, and piano-playing.

3. At the outset, some D.A. students were supported by fellowships granted by the Office of Education under the Education Professions Development Act.

4. I am glad to report that these explanations have always brought about the desired result—the hiring or promotion of the D.A. graduate.

DEGREE RECIPIENTS
THE DOCTOR OF ARTS DEGREE IN ENGLISH
THE UNIVERSITY OF MICHIGAN

December 1988

Lisa Jane McClure: Response and Revision: Informing the Writer's Process

Daniel Charles Thurber: An Approach to a Developmental English Course for Adult Cree Learners

April 1988

Christine Ann Vonder Haar: Interviewing as an Inquiry Approach in the Writing Classroom

December 1987

Cheryl Jane Burghdurf: Conversing in Communities: An Approach to Teaching Writing

Ruth Elaine Ray: Academic Literacy and Non-Native Writers

August 1987

Barbara Ellis Mirel: Text and Context: The Special Case of In-house Documentation

May 1987

William Paul Campbell: Fiction in the Composition Class: A Reorientation

Blondell Jones Freeman: Writing Anxiety: Interpersonal Views of Community College Students

December 1986

Marlene Shipp Chavis: Ten Michigan Afro-American Visual Artists: A Communality of Experience, Diversity of Means

Stephen Monroe Crow: The Works of Leslie Mormon Silko and Teaching Contemporary Native American Literature

August 1986

James Robert Saunders: Greater "Truth" in Fiction. A Study of Four Black Writers

August 1985

Mary Francis Rhodes Minock: Encompassing Discourse Polarities within a College Writing Course

May 1985

Janice Combs Epps: Literacy: The Pathway from Slavery to Freedom

M. Suzanne Lundquist: The Trickster: A Transformational Approach

December 1984

Alice Elizabeth Moorhead: The Rhetorical Design and Function of the Proposal

August 1984

Peter James Caulfield: Rhetoric and the Equal Rights Amendment: Contemporary Means of Persuasion

Miriam Rita Gannon Fabien: Using a Learning Styles Approach to Teaching Composition

Ralph Story: Master Players in a Fixed Game: An Extra-Literary History of Twentieth Century American Authors, 1896-1981

May 1984

Virginia Anne Perdue: Writing as an Act of Power: Basic Writing Pedagogy as Social Practice

Arnold Arthur Sciullo: Tolls at the Closet Doors: a Gay History for Teachers

December 1983

Alexandra Alissandratos d'Aste Surcouf: The Impact of Socio-Economic and Nationalistic Factors on the International Uses of English: A Case Study of Birzeit University

Joanna Sanders Mann: The Non-fiction of Teaching Short Fiction

Mary Pierce Quinn: Critical Thinking and Writing: An Approach to the Teaching of Composition

August 1983

Joseph David Larin: Death: In Fact, Fiction and Poetry

Richard Frank Shannon: A Small Group, Personal Growth Method for the Teaching of Writing

April 1983

James Edward Middleton: Linking Writing Instruction to Subject Area Learning: Rationale, Structures and Strategies

Rosalie Riegle Troester: Increasing Autonomy and Writing Ability: The Long-Term Effects of an Experimental Writing Course

December 1982

John David Douglass: From Yellow Creek to Somewhere

Joan Katherine Wauters: Design of a Developmental Communication Skills Program for Southeast Alaska Native College Students

August 1982

Phyllis Getschman Hastings: The Structure of Ideas in Freshman Composition

Ellen Margaret Ilfeld: Designing a Master of Arts Program in Professional Writing for Employed Adults

Andrew Lee Kelley: Hamlet and Modern Sensibilities

May 1982

Philip Erskine Brown: Paper Rappin': The Power Inclusion Model and the Politics of Voice in the Teaching of Composition

Abiodun Goke-Pariola: A Socio-Political Perspective of English Language Pedagogy in Nigerian High Schools

John Edward Sapala: Historical, Cultural, and Linguistic Aspects of Spanish-English Bilingual Education in Michigan

December 1981

Richard Alfred Malboeuf: Propositionality, Apportionality and the Writing Process

Arthur Michael Fried: Oral History in the College Composition Classroom

August 1981

Janet Grace Reusser Gilbert: Speaking and Writing Strategies: Lexicogrammatical and Behavioral Forms That Code Time and Space

Katherine Howland Harley: Theory and Practice of Writing Across the Curriculum: Humanities/Composition Link at Saginaw Valley State College, 1977-80

John Edward Martell, Jr.: Alienation, Ideology and Literature: A Marxian Pedagogy

Geneva Cobb Moore: Metamorphosis: The Shaping of Phillis Wheatley and Her Poetry

May 1981

Robert John Brockmann, Jr.: Integrating the Academic World of Technical Communications with the Commercial World of Business and Industry

December 1980

Barbara Anne Zawacki Couture: Reading to Write: An Exploration of the Uses of Analytic Reading to Teach Composition

Ruth E. Rubin Goldman: The Teaching and Learning of

Reading in the Community College: Why—How—Under What Conditions?

August 1980

Richard James Follett: On Teaching Gay Literature

Barbara Jean Hunt: Establishing and Implementing a Writing Center on the College Level

May 1980

Paul Gregory Bator: The Impact of Cognitive Development Upon Audience Awareness in the Writing Process

Gregory Lee Flynn: Reading, Thinking and Writing: A Practical Rhetoric with Readings

Paula Diane Rubenstein: Communications Theory and Pedagogy for Working Women in Organizational Structure

August 1979

John David Beard: Toward a Rationale for Analyzing Writing in Peer Groups

April 1979

Melba Joyce Boyd: Visual Perception and the Teaching of English

Edward Thomas Hill: Personal Writing: A Developmental Writing Program for Clarity of Communication Through Self-Direction

Lawrence Barton Boyer: The General Studies Program: A Proposal for an Interdisciplinary Cluster College at the Community College Featuring the Use of Small Groups for

Courses in the Development of Human Potential and English Composition

December 1978

Robert James Allan: Writing: A Creative Venture into the Psycho-Dynamics of Mind

Terrance Michael Skelton: Career-Oriented Communication: Determining the Instructional Needs of the Community College Vocational-Technical Student

August 1978

Mildred Bauman Krnacik: Egocentrism in the Written and Oral Production of Freshman Composition Students

December 1977

Herman Lamar Bingham: Effective Writing in the English Classroom vis-a-vis Instructional Media

John LeRoy Doty: Becoming Visually Perceptive: An Introduction to the Art of the Film

Horace Still Newsum: The Politics of "Scholarship" in Black Intellectual Discourse: Writing as Writers

Richard John Prince: To Arrive Where We Started: Archetypes of the American Eden in Popular Culture

Frederick LeRoy Salsman: Unmelted Composition: A Multi-Cultural Approach to Teaching English Composition in an Urban Setting

Lennie Donald Stanciel: Speech-Comp: English Composition in the Introductory Speech Class

Gerald Charles Van Dusen: Teaching the Process of Editing

August 1977

Marilynn Powe Bell: Using the Black Female Autobiography to Teach Freshman College English

Shannon Kelly Butler: Language as Play: Teaching Composition Through Gaming

Ted Charles Jennings: Take a Sad Song

Jeffrey Lee Weisberg: The Motivations and Effects of Daily Creative Writing

May 1977

Beverly Virginia Head: Pre-Writing: The Discovery State in Writing

Majorie Ashton Oliver: Styles of Illocutionary Action: Speech Acts and the Study of Comedy and Tragedy

Kathleen Lee Eisele: Writing Security

Edith Morris Croake: The Evolution and Description of a Process for Planning an Effective Composition Course

December 1976

Jeffrey Jay Butler: The Process of Composition: Model, Strategies and Sources

Ann Marie Green: Writing in the Community

August 1976

Raymond Dell Spitzenberger: English Intervention Programs

in Higher Education: Discourse by Research, by Journal, by Drama

Daniel Richard Thomas: Toward a Rhetoric

May 1976

Inelda Celina Howard: Psychological and Methodological Considerations in the Second Language Classroom from the Learner's Perspective

Douglas Andrew Stauffer: Using Programmed Materials to Teach English

December 1975

Gary Nelson Christensen: Theme-A-Day: An Evaluation of the Effectiveness of Daily Practice in a College Composition Course

F. Sharon Drolet: Transactional Analysis and Related Psychotherapeutic Techniques in the College Composition and Communication Classroom

Alberta Darlene Goodman: Utilization of Positive Feedback in a Classroom Environment of Acceptance to Promote Enhanced Learner Self-Concept and Improved Written Performance

Joan Marie Martin: American Literature: Towards a Redefinition

Consuela Marie Moore: The Tri-Colored Caged Muse: A Comparative Study of Afro-American, Mexican-American, and Native-American Literature

Mark Edward Smith: Peer Tutoring in a Writing Workshop

August 1975

James Michael Brazil: On Teaching Composition at the Community College

Mark Keith Edmonds: Reading/Writing

Jacqueline Anita Jones: Communicating in Writing: A Rhetorical Model for Developing Composition Skills

Sr. Madeleine Kisner: Color in the Worlds and Works of Poe, Hawthorne, Crane, Anderson and Welty

Carl James Koch: Small Groups in the Composition Class: A Case Study of Developing Linguistic Security and Written Fluency

Sara Ann Lincoln: A Feminist Process in Teaching: A Personal Account

Katherine Bernice Payant Pavlik: The Use of Visual Media and Popular Culture in Teaching English Composition

May 1975

James Arthur Odom: Considerations for Change in Community College English Instructional Programs

Ruth Jett Staton: Crossing the Wine Dark Sea of Broadcasting

December 1974

Edward Anderson: Dimensions of Language and Rhetorical Styles in Black America

Susan McMurray Anderson: Metaphoric Dimensions Myth in an Interdisciplinary Context

Gloria Maria De Feo Kitto: American Arts in Perspective

Thomas Mathew Rivers: A Metacritical and Interdisciplinary Approach to Teaching Appreciation of the Arts

August 1974

Barbara Smith Morris: A College Workshop for Performing Arts and Media Study

May 1974

Catherine Elizabeth Frerichs Lamb: On Suffering Change: Toward a Theory of Instruction in the Art of Invention

December 1973

Stephen Dale Chennault: Silence is Black: Black Attitudes in an Urban Classroom

Donald Coonley: Individual Insights into Writing

John Maury Dean: Pop-Rock Comp: Resurrection of Freshman English

Virgil Glen Gulker: The Penal English Course

Bernard Joseph Reilly: Reading and Writing in the Community College: Building Upon Tacit Linguistic Knowledge

Darrel Wayne Staat: Technological Literacy: The Student as Inventor

Paul William Swets: Experimental Research in Teaching Rhetoric

The D.A. in English at Illinois State University

WILLIAM C. WOODSON
Director of Graduate Studies
(Department of English)
Illinois State University

Founded in 1857, Illinois State University was a nationally recognized teacher's college until the late 50s, when the Illinois Board of Higher Education gave ISU a new mission—to become a multi-purpose university. To prepare for this expansion, buildings were built and departments grew; enrollment climbed steadily from 5,000 to 15,000 in a decade. The faculty in English more than doubled to 65 professors, drawn from schools across the country. In 1971 Don Cameron Allen visited the department and encouraged us to prepare to offer the Ph.D.

Over the next few years, the department prepared several trial programs, but none gained university support. The financial crunch meanwhile caught ISU in its jaws. At this juncture, when things looked grim, a new president came to ISU, Gene Budig, convinced that the D.A. was the perfect degree for a former teacher's training school to offer. Under his leadership, four D.A.s were instituted during the 1970s, in Mathematics, History, English, and Economics.

The D.A. in English was approved in 1975 and we recruited the first class, primarily among community college teachers; our first graduate was hooded in 1980. By the time this essay sees print, we will have graduated nearly 50 D.A.s. Graduates are teaching on several continents and at a variety of colleges and universities across America. In 1987, half the doctorates in English from public universities in Illinois were D.A.s. We expect to graduate 6-8 candidates a year for the foreseeable future.

The design of the D.A. program at ISU is an important reason for the success we have had. Although we offer a generalist's degree, we structured the D.A. somewhat differently from other D.A. programs. Ray Lewis White, a literary scholar and today a Distinguished University Professor, chaired the graduate committee which designed the degree. He believed from the outset that the degree must integrate the study of literature with the study of language, composition, and pedagogy, if it were to address the teaching skills needed in most college classrooms and simultaneously draw from the research interests of the graduate faculty. Moreover, he argued that the degree should have a strong research base, culminating in a rigorous dissertation.

The aim from the outset was to put theory into practice in the classroom. Most dissertations have grown out of experimental teaching internships, and the majority of them have examined closely ways to improve the way students write or read, recently including the relationship between reading and writing. Because all of the composition courses at ISU are now taught on computers, dissertations have begun to theorize that practice too.

The department has followed the degree in its staffing, so that over the past fifteen years we have become a nearly balanced department, with half the faculty in literature, the rest in the other areas of our discipline. The chairperson, Charles Harris, made a strong commitment to building the D.A. program when he assumed departmental leadership in 1978; he too is a literary scholar, as am I.

The degree has not divided the department into camps; indeed, because there is a 5 member dissertation committee, and because dissertation proposals must be approved by a large graduate committee, a majority of the graduate faculty has been directly involved with the program since its inception. With research bibliographies for dissertation proposals typically running 20 pages or more, candidates have been publishing along the way to completion, a pleasing outcome for the faculty and a necessity in the job market.

A full-time student who teaches two courses a semester can

finish coursework in two years, counting summer session. Our typical summer offerings for 1989 include 15 graduate courses, to accommodate students who attend primarily in the summers—and also the workaholics who want to make progress through the coursework as rapidly as possible.

We recruit nationally, seeking apt students who have a demonstrated commitment to and talent for college teaching. The four-year colleges and regional universities have discovered the need for "general practioners" of English in reaction to the astounding drop-out rates of the freshmen who don't know how to learn, and the sophomores who are only wise fools. These general practioner D.A.s do not rely merely on intuition, commitment, and integrity as teaching techniques; these D.A.s will also bring to the classroom a storehouse of research into reading, writing, language, and learning theory.

The Research Component in the Doctor of Arts Degree

FRANK GINANNI
Chair, English Department
Middle Tennessee State University

A narrative history of the Doctor of Arts program at Middle Tennessee State University should be helpful to our purpose because the changes in the program were central to the research components in the total curriculum as well as in the design of individual courses. Initiated in 1970, the Doctor of Arts program at Middle Tennessee State University offered degrees in three disciplines: English, History and Physical Education. The stated purpose of the degree was to train "senior college, community college, and junior college teacher-scholars" in those three fields. The rationale for selecting English, History and Physical Education was simply that those three disciplines were at the core of any lower-division, General Studies program, whether at community college, junior college, or four-year institution. Thus, it was thought, the need for teachers in basic courses would remain stable and constant. It was easy to feel so confident about the constant demand for instructors in 1970; we were, after all, in an expansionist mode. What is implicit in such a description and rationale, but is nowhere explicitly stated by the university, is that we were concentrating on training students to teach basic courses at the lower-division level. Nowhere was it officially stated that holders of the D.A. degree would be trained to teach specialized upper-division courses to majors in the discipline; however, it was widely speculated that if they taught at four-year institutions, they would be required—and willing—to do so. Any suggestion that holders of the D.A. might be competent to teach at the graduate level was immediately dismissed.

Even a brief look at a summary of the curriculum for the

D.A. degree as it was originally designed should make it clear why the English faculty drew the inferences it did about the purposes of the program and our responsibilities to students and to their employers, current or prospective. As initially designed, the D.A. degree required 59 hours beyond the M.A. distributed in the following manner: a 15 semester hour core in Higher Education; a 20 semester hour requirement in English, of which 2 hours were for two semesters of internship experience, leaving 18 hours of course work. And only two courses had to come from a series of four specially designed in contemporary literature at the doctoral level. There was also an academic minor of 12 hours required. Finally, 12 hours for the dissertation brought the total to 59. Clearly, then, 18 hours of course work beyond a master's degree did not, in our judgment, adequately train a student to teach either specialized upper-division courses or graduate level courses of any nature.

At the publication of the Graduate Bulletin two years later, the distribution of those 59 semester hours had been revised, primarily as a consequence of the dissatisfaction of English and History faculty. (Except to say that the D.A. degree was the President's pet project, I shall not at this time rehearse for you the wars that ensued between the President and faculty when we had the temerity to express our dissatisfaction with the academic integrity of the curriculum.) Back to its revision. The major was increased to 26 hours, but still included 2 hours for the internship. The net gain in course work in the major was thus 6 hours. This was accomplished by reducing the Higher Education core from 15 to 12 hours. The minor stayed the same at 12 hours. Another revision of the curriculum was made approximately five years later, and it remains the one we have today. Two alternative routes to the degree were provided: a 48 hour program without an academic minor and a 60 hour program with two teaching fields. The 48 hour program consists of a major of 24 hours of course work, plus 6 hours of internship/externship, plus 6 hours of dissertation. The remaining 12 hours come from a core of professional education courses. The 60 hour alternative consists of 18 hours of course work in a major, 18 hours in a related teaching field, 6 of internship/externship, 6 of dissertation, and 12 in professional education.

One further change was made in D.A. offerings in 1982 when proposals for D.A. degrees in Chemistry and Economics were approved. As of December 17, 1988, Middle Tennessee State has awarded 175 D.A. degrees, forty-seven of which were in English. The English department, then, accounts for 27% of D.A. degrees awarded. To my knowledge, all but two of those are currently employed in education, and one of those two has been, at times, a part-time instructor. I must quickly add, however, that most of our students come to us during summer sessions or in night graduate programs, and those students are already employed. I estimate that 90% of our D.A. students fall under this category. We have accommodated these students with special circumstances by allowing residency to be established during three summer sessions. Further, we encourage prospective students from surrounding states by offering several summer fellowships. They cover out-of-state fees which are above tuition remitted. That figure amounts to about $500. The rest can be used for dormitory room rent and board for a ten week summer session.

The D.A. program in English differs from those of the four other disciplines in only one significant respect, and that difference is to our point here as we consider the research element in D.A. programs and research/publication requirements for D.A. holders. The D.A. program in English at M.T.S.U. gives students three dissertation options. The dissertation may be A) a problem in the student's major field aimed at specific curriculum development; B) research into or critical analysis of a body of literary materials; or C) an interdisciplinary dissertation. In case A, the dissertation committee should be composed of members from English and education; in case B, the committee may be composed solely of members of the English Department; in case C, the committee should be composed of members from English, the related field, and education. Of the 47 degrees awarded in English, only 6 have been option A, pedagogical in purpose.

One early in the program was an interdisciplinary work; all others have dealt with a research project into a specific body of literary materials.

The other four departments refer the student to the description of the dissertation found in the Graduate Catalog. Briefly, it describes a research project strongly based upon the discipline but having some relevance to teaching undergraduates; its scope should be so limited as to allow completion within six months; it should be a synthesis of the discipline and professional experiences in courses, seminars, and the internship; it should demonstrate an understanding of teaching, instruction, and curriculum, related to the discipline but looking to the organization and interpretation of knowledge rather than the discovery of new knowledge. Clearly, then, the intention is to give students a program which strongly emphasizes the relationship between an academic discipline and professional education courses in pedagogy to train them for teaching undergraduates. Nowhere in the description of the program is there an expressed purpose to train our students to conduct research projects for professional presentation or publication. In fact, the language in the Graduate Catalog appears to discourage such activity.

However, from the inception of the program we in the English department reasoned—correctly, I think—that the nature of literary studies at the graduate level requires not only a strong research and writing component in each course, but also an equally strong individual bibliography and research course within the program. Further, we reasoned that whether our graduates taught at the high school, community college, junior college or four year institution, their promotion, tenure, and merit pay evaluations would be enhanced if they participated in professional organizations, made presentations and read papers at conferences, and published results of their independent research. Administrators, we suggest, approve of such professional activities even though written policies do not explicitly require such activities.

Although we have done no careful follow-up studies which would document the professional research activities of our graduates, we have a wealth of anecdotal material because many of our graduates teach within a few hundred mile radius of middle Tennessee. Consequently, we see them frequently at state and regional conferences, or individual faculty members correspond with former students and keep us posted on their activities. We learn, of course, that our graduates participate in professional organizations, conduct research projects, read papers at conferences and sometimes publish. All of this is done without release time or with little financial support from their institutions. Many of these people teach fifteen hour loads of freshman and sophomore courses, but they choose to remain active scholars and writers in addition to their many non-instructional responsibilities. They continue to participate in these activities because they retain an interest in literary studies as valuable enterprise in itself. We like to think that our graduates' continuing interest in their discipline is partly a consequence of their graduate experience in our department. On the whole, then, we feel reasonably comfortable with the academic experiences we have provided our students, given a program in which only half the required hours may be taken in courses from the student's major area. We hope that we have helped prepare them to respond to the changing demands made on them by institutions which themselves are almost constantly undergoing change. Those demands, often unspoken and almost never written, increasingly require our graduates to engage in research and publication.

History and Description of the Interdisciplinary D.A. in History, St. John's Uuniverity

FRANK J. COPPA
Director, D.A. History
St. John's University

I was involved with the Doctor of Arts Degree for some ten years, examining programs at various schools, nationwide.[1] Later, I helped draft the program for the Doctor of Arts in Modern World History at St. John's University. More recently, I have served as a faculty member and director of our Doctor of Arts program which was launched the fall of 1986. In this decade of D.A. involvement, I have been barraged by a series of queries about the degree in general, and our program in particular. The most frequently asked questions are: What is the D.A. degree? How does the D.A. differ from the Ph.D.? and most often, Is it for me?

Together these questions formed the focus of the joint session of the Modern Language Association and the Council of National Literatures held in New Orleans, December 28, 1988. I examined how the D.A. differs from the Ph.D. by concentrating on one of the unique features of the degree: its interdisciplinary nature. I did so by examining the history and development of the D.A. and by commenting on the interdisciplinary Doctor of Arts in Modern World History offered at St. John's.

the Doctor of Arts resulted from the critical evaluation of graduate education in the 1960s, and the criticism of the training received by those who sought positions in community colleges and four year programs. Few, if any, graduate departments admitted they were in large part training future college teachers.[2] Small wonder their graduates knew little about teaching, nor were trained to teach. Yet, most graduates of these traditional programs eventually found themselves in the classroom. The National Endowment for the Humanities report on higher education in the 1980s noted that "many graduate schools have become so preoccupied with training narrow research specialists that they no longer address adequately the more pressing need of higher education for good teachers."[3] Concomitantly, there has been a mounting criticism of the academic training, parochialism, and professional qualifications of secondary school teachers.[4] In light of these considerations a broader, less research-oriented liberal arts doctoral degree was sought for college teachers.

The D.A. or "teaching doctorate" discussed as an alternative for decades, came of age in 1968 when Carnegie-Mellon awarded the first degree. Within two years, the Council of Graduate Schools recommended the establishment of programs leading to the Doctor of Arts to prepare students for effective teaching, and guidelines were elaborated.[5]

As of 1980, and the last nationwide survey of the Doctor of Arts, there were twenty-six institutions granting the degree, collectively offering twenty-eight majors. The most frequently offered were English (13). History (7), Chemistry (6), Mathematics (6) and Biology (4). The same 1980 survey revealed that 39 percent of the holders of the degree were employed in four year colleges, 23 percent by universities, 22 percent in community colleges and 16 percent in secondary schools, government, and business. The D.A. continues to appeal to prospective teachers.[6]

St. John's University, long dedicated to the Humanities, has always attracted those interested in teaching. Thus the Doctor of Arts program was a natural consequence. Presently the University has has two Doctor of Arts Programs in place. The English program introduced in 1979; the one in Modern World history in 1986. Both are interdisciplinary, although to a different degree.

In its 1970 statement the Council emphasized that the Ph.D. should be the highest research degree; the D.A. would emphasize teaching. As evolved in the 1970s the Doctor of Arts was designed not to replace, but to parallel, existing Ph.D.

programs and oriented towards developing teacher competence in a broad subject matter area. To assure comprehensive coverage, a broad course selection which might bridge several disciplines, was recommended. This would transcend the specialization found within most Ph.D. programs. There was also a call for functional foreign language and research tools; a research component that would have practical applicability in the classroom; a supervised internship or its equivalent to improve teaching, and finally a less specialized comprehensive than generally found within Ph.D. programs.[7]

A primary difference between the D.A. and the Ph.D. is the purpose and scope of the research in the respective degrees. As in all doctoral programs, the D.A. requires a strong research component. However this has a focus and intensity different from that for the Ph.D., which results in a dissertation and the discovery of new knowledge. Within the D.A. research is seen to lead to an enhancement of scholarly knowledge, and its application in the classroom.[8]

In January 1971 the Regents of New York authorized the granting of the Doctor of Arts. The guidelines adopted incorporated most of the features outlined by the Council of Graduate Schools and the D.A. granting institutions.[9] In the State's revised guidelines (1975), the Regents announced that the Doctor of Arts degree presumed a more comprehensive knowledge and broader course work than is generally the case with the Ph.D. In addition to the earlier requirements, New York State stressed the need to provide a broad education not only for teachers but for people in business, government agencies, and other areas.[10]

To assure comprehensive coverage a large course selection from a number of disciplines was suggested. The determination to widen the scope of the subject area as well as research solved the problem of parochialism, but threatened the coherence of the program. A smorgasbord of choice, encouraged by the supermarket approach to education, could create confusion.[11] To counter this possible problem, the D.A. granting institutions stressed the need for a problem or theme approach in those degree programs based on two or more disciplines.[12] A program that incorporates varied material required some conceptual framework. Those of us involved in the Doctor of Arts in Modern World History at St. John's decided upon the theme of global interdependence, flowing from modernization.

Within the current restructuring of education in general, and history programs in particular, there has been a call for relevance. We have witnessed an appreciation of the global dimension of past and current developments, a recognition of the limits of the older diplomatic and political approach to history, and the need to include economic, social, philosophical, and religious dimensions, transcending the narrower approach of the traditional Ph.D. programs.[13] These elements figure prominently in the D.A. in Modern World History.

The need to transcend an outdated, parochial perspective is real.[14] The report of the Commission headed by Clark Kerr, "The United States Prepares for its Future: Global Perspective in Education" found that America's schoolchildren are "globally illiterate," lacking a knowledge of the culture, history, and geography of other peoples and nations. The Commission recognized that the teaching profession would have to be upgraded to realize the goals which it deems essential for the future.[15] "We cannot hope to understand . . . twentieth century dilemmas with nineteenth-century curricula," writes Shirley Hufstedler, Secretary of Education, "Our educators are going to have to take a hard new look at what they are teaching—and not teaching—about the world.[16] This was confirmed by the 25 member Commission on Foreign Languages and International Studies in the late 1970's which was "profoundly alarmed" by the results of its inquiry.[17]

We are living in an unprecedented period. For the first time people all over the world, regardless of differences in language, culture, religion, way of life, and past experience are compressed into an inescapable interaction. Financial markets have a worldwide impact; recessions cannot be confined by borders. Citing transformations in science, communication, and above all, military technology, Mikhail Gorbachev, speaking before the General Assembly of the United Nations on December

7, 1988, aptly described the present age as radically different from even the recent past. Addressing the global community on the need to preserve our universal civilization, the Secretary General called for a basic restructuring of political and economic international relations, replacing unilateralism with multilateralism.[18]

Certainly in our age of global confluence, old perspectives are no longer germane: the strategies of individual people living in separate cultural units no longer suffice. Contemporary history is global history; national history, considered in isolation, no longer makes sense.

Our program recognizes that sensible history must have a global perspective, stressing the interdependence of the five billion human beings sharing one planet. The approach is interdisciplinary because man is a social and economic being, as well as a political one, and is shaped by a multiplicity of forces including philosophy and religion. We, too, have found that world issues cannot be compartmentalized by departmental divisions.[19] We are not alone. Within the past decade historians in the United States have demonstrated an increased willingness to address issues on an interdisciplinary plane.[20] Our curriculum aims to prepare teachers and other leaders for a world shaped by global events and the greater interaction produced by the march of modernization.

Because of the world scope of such problems as population growth, disease, adequate food, housing, and energy, as well as the hazards of environmental pollution, we settled upon the theme of global interdependence for our program. To understand the importance of this new international interdependence we consider it necessary to examine its historical, cultural, philosophical and religious dimension as well as the cross fertilization and similarities among past and contemporary civilizations. This program stresses global interdependence from the Age of the Atlantic Revolution to our present period of technological innovation. It provides a curriculum that will enable teachers to improve their understanding of international affairs and world history, and transmit this to their students.

Students in the program are introduced to the principal academic area by two team taught, interdisciplinary seminars which focus respectively on "Patterns of Modernization in Historical Perspective," and the "International Implications of Modernization." The seminars are team rather than sequentially taught.[21] These comparative seminars, which point out the weaknesses of a one-sided national perspective and limited cultural solutions, are central to the program. They provide the two-fold division for coursework. There is also a Concluding Seminar, again taught by faculty with different specialities but shared interests, which serves to integrate the earlier course work while relating the material to the professional skill area. These team-taught seminars expose their participants to various ways of observing the historical process, enabling them to develop an integrated humanistic understanding. They also focus on the avalanche of problems confronting humanity, and call for new priorities and perspectives in understanding the contemporary global confluence.

The core faculty for the program is drawn from the departments of history, anthropology, sociology, philosophy, government and politics, and theology, among others. Nonetheless, history remains the core discipline in this interdisciplinary program providing an integrating approach, at once humanistic and social scientific, to the study of international affairs and problems. The team taught, interdisciplinary seminars provide an arena for dialogue between the humanistic and social scientific approaches providing both theoretical insights and practical solutions.

Currently the value of this broadly conceived and interdisciplinary degree is demonstrated by the changes being suggested in university curriculums such as exposing students to a wider variety of courses and a greater number of minors, the steady increase in non-Western studies, and the replacement of western civilization by world history courses in many colleges. Similar trends are discernible in the high schools. In New York State, for example, the emphasis in social studies is on global interaction with the new curriculum seeking to inculcate global awareness among the students.[22] The D.A.

with its practical rather than theoretical emphasis, with its broad, interdisciplinary course-work as well as specific emphasis on improving and introducing new teaching methods, is an ideal degree for teachers at the secondary, community college, and university level.[23]

During the next decade when the educational establishment will have to introduce far-reaching changes, the holder of the D.A. will be ideally prepared. This degree's broad focus, emphasis on interdisciplinarity, concern with cultural pluralism and innovative teaching will give its holders a decided advantage. Indeed the D.A. graduate will be prepared to assume a leadership role in introducing changes, more so than the holder of the more narrowly focused Ph.D. The D.A. will also play an important role in forging institutional and instructional links between the secondary schools and the universities, which is long overdue.

NOTES

1. For an evaluation of the degree see Arthur M. Eastman (ed.), *Proceedings of the Wingspread Conference on the Doctor of Arts Degree, October 25-27, 1970* (Washington, D.C. Council of Graduate Schools in the United States, 1970) and Paul L. Dressel and Mary M. Thompson, "The Doctor of Arts: A Decade of Development, 1967-1977," *Journal of History of Education*, 49 (1978), 329-336.

2. Edmond L. Volpe, "A portrait of the Ph.D. As a Failure," *Bulletin of the Association of Department of English*, November, 1970, p. 4.

3. "To Reclaim a Legacy: A Report on the Humanities in Higher Education."

4. Charles Silberman, *Crisis in the Classroom*. (New York: Random House, 1970); J. Boyd Page (ed.), "Preface," *Scholarship for Society: Panel on Alternate Approaches to Graduate Education*. (Princeton, N.J.: Educational Testing Service, 1973).

5. "The Doctor of Arts Degree: A Proposal for Guidelines," (Committee on Graduate Studies of the American Association of State Colleges and Universities, 1970).

6. A. William Johnson, "Current Status of the Doctor of Arts: A Decade of Development," *Communicator*, XIII (December, 1980), n. 4; James G. Hunt and David L. Wheeler, "Survey of the Status of the Doctor of Arts Degree in the United States 1980," Ball State University, 1980.

7. "The Doctor of Arts Degree: A Statement by The Council of Graduate Schools in the United States," 1970.

8. *Ibid.;* "Supplementary Statement on the Doctor of Arts Degree," The Council of Graduate Schools in the United States, 1972.

9. For the latter see "Draft on the D.A. by D.A. Granting Institutions," 1979 and "The Doctor of Arts Degree: A Degree for College Teachers. Prepared by representatives of thirteen D.A. granting institutions." Michigan State University Printing, February 28, 1980.

10. *New York State Education Department News*, September 26, 1975.

11. Scott Heller, "A New Wave of Curricular R form: Connections Between Disciplines," *The Chronicle of Higher Education*, September 2, 1987, p. 28; Edward B. Fiske, "3-Year Survey Finds College Curriculums In U.S. in 'Disarray'," *The New York Times*, February 11, 1985.

12. Johnson, *Communicator*, XIII (December, 1980), n. 4.

13. Theodore H. Von Loue, "Responsibility Over Mindset," The American Historical Association's *Perspective*, January, 1988, pp. 15-16.

14. "Internationalizing the Curriculum," *National Forum*, Fall, 1988.

15. Clark Kerr, "Education for Global Perspectives," *The Annals of the American Academy of Political and Social Science*, vol. 442, (March 1979), 112; Cyrus R. Vance, "The End of Innocence," *Education and the World View*, Change Magazine Press, 1980.

16. Shirley M. Hufstedler, "A World In Transition," *Educating for the World View*. (New Rochelle, N.Y. Council on Learning, 1980).

17. John Brademas, "Growing Up Internationally: America Faces Global Realities," *Educational Record*, Spring, 1987, p. 8.

18. *The New York Times*, December 8, 1988, p. A,16.

19. Pat Watters, "The Interdisciplinary Umbrella," *Educating for The World View*, p. 62.

20. Majorie Lightman, "The Emergence of An Independent Scholarly Sector: History as a Case Study,: *Outside Academe: New Ways of Working in the Humanities*. New York: The Institute for Research in History, 1981. p. 6.

21. For an explanation and analysis of the distinction see Rivers Singleton, Jr. "Interdisciplinary Teaching with Humanities," *Perspectives in Biology and Medicine*, Winter, 1983, pp. 304-306.

22. Fred M. Hechingher, "Council to Fight U.S. Student's Parochial View," *The New York Times*, March 13, 1979.

23. Volpe, *Bulletin of the Association of Departments of English*, November, 1980, pp. 5-6.

The D.A. at the Community College: Research for the Future

GEORGE L. GROMAN

Fiorello H. LaGuardia Community College

(The City University of New York)

The Doctor of Arts degree continues to flourish and has become an important component of higher education in the United States. Indeed, as a visiting professor in St. John's D.A. Program in English, I have observed its progress firsthand. Additionally, as a faculty member at a community college and (for twelve years) as a department and division chairman of Humanities, I have faced the problems and challenges many a D.A. graduate will confront. It is my view that well-designed D.A. programs can and will provide faculty urgently needed in the 1990's and beyond. Moreover, the most ambitious, energetic, and creative of these D.A. graduates can find in the changing needs of undergraduate education both personal fulfillment and professional recognition.

Much useful research can be done at the community college where problems and challenges are plentiful—as a brief profile of the community college student will suggest. Today a community college student is most often the first in his or her family to be enrolled in a college, is often a high school graduate with a GED, is somewhat more likely to be female than male, is often from a minority background, and may be foreign born. Such a student comes to college with very limited financial resources and with few, if any, of the financial and social cushions available to the middle-class student when disaster strikes. As many studies point out, the entering community college student may suffer from low self-esteem and harbor many insecurities about his or her ability to succeed in a college setting (Gittell 54). A college degree is viewed as a ticket to enhanced career or job possibilities and a somewhat more secure financial future.

The classroom teacher needs to understand the student's concerns and also respect his or her goals, but at the same time will seek to offer a wider range of possibilities for study and reflection. In the area of basic skills in English, of course much important work has already been done. We might point to Mina Shaughnessy's now classic book *Errors and Expectations* as well as to the work of such thoughtful writers as Peter Elbow, Ken Bruffee, Wayne Booth, and Harvey Wiener. There has been much experimentation with media, particularly with the use of film (Cohn 32), and, most recently, with the computer (Gallagher). It is, in any case, clear that if the community college student is to succeed in basic skills areas, much careful support must be provided—through counselling, through tutoring, through the use of such strategies as collaborative learning, and through *thoughtful* use of the equipment which science and technology provide and will continue to provide. The new D.A. who is the graduate of a well-integrated program (including supervised internships and research specifically directed to student needs) will already have a head start in the areas indicated (Thompson 2-4). In some ways, such research is always fresh because times change, student populations change, the demands of the job market change, attitudes toward language change, and because technology usually advances more quickly than does our ability to adjust to it. The computer itself symbolizes for students an approach to mainstream activities and a gateway to professionalism. There is a gripping interaction between the computer and the student and between and among students as they come to discover for themselves that writing is a process as well as a product and as they "publish" by means of a printer. Much work is still to be done on the strategies for the use of this remarkable machine and in the development of appropriate software for the writing classroom.

Skills mastery or competence may represent a beginning with content a vital second or later stage of learning. Although it is not my primary purpose here to argue the relative merits or placement of skills or content courses, it is useful at least to note that the much inflated controversy surrounding this issue is bound to affect educational research for some time to come. Harvey Wiener, now a dean at the City University of New York's central headquarters, argues that despite the popularity of such "conservative" critics as E. D. Hirsch, "the purpose of education resides less in the notion of giving students information about the world than in giving them ways to understand the world" (Wiener 8). Hirsch, of course, argues just the reverse—that the skills training without essential information about the world and significant concepts that affect contemporary attitudes and values leaves the student or graduate unable to function in today's society. Although Hirsch's list of essentials (152-215) may not represent a miraculous solution (as he himself readily admits), it does seem, at least to me, a step in the right direction. Our high school and college graduates should know that there was an American Revolution and that it represented a sharp political departure from the past, that the Constitution with its Bill of Rights was a remarkable and important document, that the Civil War, the two world conflagrations in this century, along with the Korean and Vietnamese conflicts, changed the course of world history as did Pontius Pilate and the use of penicillin. I confess it troubles me that recently a student at a reputable college could respond to a question about the Holocaust by saying that she believed it was some sort of a Jewish holiday. Perhaps, after all, most educators do believe, along with Professor Alan Bloom (*Closing of the American Mind*), that *some* sorts of information are essential—though the kinds and extent will obviously differ.

At the community college, there will be less concern with research that leads to the building of a traditional list or a literary canon than with assembling a group of works that will be significant and at the same time *accessible* to groups of students with varying skills and widely differing backgrounds. To be sure, cultural and ethnic diversity in the classroom can be valuable, leading to all kinds of insights, but at the same time can prove difficult for the instructor seeking to suggest a commonality of interests and concerns.

In a recent class of my own, I had a student from Vietnam, another from Taiwan, a Palestinian Arab, foreign-born Hispanics, and American-born black students. Happily, they came to know and respect one another and, I hope, the instructor as well. What held us together was a shared writing experience and a focus on specific artistic works. The search for such works is critical both in the individual classroom and in large programmatic terms. I myself have come to realize recently that those students who have been in the United States for only a short time often are concerned not so much with race, ethnicity, and gender (certainly areas of current discussion) as they are with the immediate problem of survival. Perhaps a book such as Defoe's *Robinson Crusoe* may not be an appropriate text in every respect, but sections of the book do suggest the determination of someone bent on surviving, individual resourcefulness, the possibilities for adaptation, and the ways in which an individual's cultural past continues to affect the present. I might add one other example, D. H. Lawrence's "The Rocking-Horse Winner," which I have used several times in the classroom. In the story, an English, middle-class boy who can, on occasion, predict the outcome of horse races is determined to assist his financially troubled family, and in wrestling with adult problems somewhat beyond his understanding, he focuses again and again on the concept of *luck*, finally investing it with magical properties. Yet when I asked the members of one class to define luck in their own way, the answer was quite different: luck meant surviving day to day and reaching home without being mugged! In this case as in the previous one, students articulated their own concerns and at the same time reached for different responses through the magic medium of literature.

Perhaps our own luck as administrators, faculty members, and researchers is in having the chance to test and retest our own perceptions and to serve students with large needs and big dreams. The D.A. who opts for a career at the community college will certainly have a special kind of luck that includes the opportunity to do a great deal of teaching and research that really matters.

WORKS CITED

Bloom, Allan. *The Closing of the American Mind.* New York: Touchstone, 1988.

Cohn, Jan. "A D.A. Program for Inservice Training of Teachers in Two-Year Colleges." *Teaching English in the Two-Year College* Spring 1976: 32-35.

Gallagher, Brian. *Microcomputers and Word Processing Programs: an Evaluation and Critique.* New York: City University of New York, 1985.

Gittell, Marilyn. "Reaching the Hard to Reach." *Change* 17 Sept.-Oct. 1985: 51-60.

Hirsch, E. D. *Cultural Literacy: What Every American Needs to Know.* New York: Vintage, 1988: 152-215.

Thompson, Mary Magdala. "History and Update of the Doctor of Arts Program." *Colorado Journal of Education* Spring 1978: 2-6.

Reflections on the Doctor of Arts

BRUCE K. MARTIN
Chair, English Department
Drake University

When I received the invitation to appear on a panel concerned with the status and future of the Doctor of Arts degree, I was more than a little amused, since its status at Drake University is dwindling daily and its future there will be brief: the phasing out of our D.A. program began three years ago, no new candidates have been accepted since then, most who had been accepted before have finished the degree, while a few yet remaining are working on dissertations. Thus, as I explained to Professor Paolucci, I have little by way of a live program to describe, and what little else I can say on this subject might inform or please no one at today's meeting. But, because she seemed to feel otherwise, here I am.

My amusement is compounded by this being another of a series of events tying *me* in particular to the fortunes of the D.A. It is true that I have been on the Drake University faculty now for over twenty years, and that I was present at the inception of the Drake D.A. in English in the early 1970s. But, as a very-junior faculty member, I was hardly in a position either to influence the decision to set up such a program or to help determine the specific shape which it initially took at Drake. Along with a number of others in the department more-or-less just out of graduate school, I felt pretty much on the sidelines as the senior folks put this thing together. Its momentum had come from university and department factors put in motion before I and the other junior people had arrived, and most of us were pretty much caught up in the beginnings of our careers as teachers and members of a new and still strange university environment.

Though each of us held varying feelings toward the program

being put in place in the name of the department which we
had recently joined, none was hostile toward it. And even
the strongest skeptics soon admitted that the D.A. permitted
us to teach courses we might not have otherwise taught and
introduced us to students whom we probably could not have
taught without Drake having the D.A.—including some
extraordinary people who, I am sure, could have done well
in the best Ph.D. programs in English. At least to the extent
that we benefited personally from such arrangements, we all
became supportive of the program. And as time passed and
as I and my contemporaries participated in the administering
and refining of the program, we ceased being strangers to
its workings. Even so, after I became department chairman
in 1983, and thus to that extent especially responsible for
the program, and particularly a year later, when I had to
begin answering for the program to a university-wide strategic
planning panel, some of whom had long been hostile toward
it, the irony of this once-outsider having to take on such
tasks was certainly not lost on me. My speaking to you today
is thus another piece of the same ironic pattern.

I am not interested in rehearsing for you the process by
which Drake got in, stayed in, and is getting out of the D.A.
business or in digging up either the original feelings
surrounding our program or those which replaced them. To
do so would be mostly to point to institutional factors and
to particular decisions and decision-makers more-or-less
peculiar to Drake and therefore of little bearing on your
situations. Nor am I interested in encouraging or discouraging
you from having or maintaining your particular D.A.
programs. Certainly not the latter, since last year our
department went on a hiring binge by bringing in persons
in five newly defined positions, two of whom are D.A.s—
we continue to consider it a viable credential. However, I
would like you to imagine with me a sort of Rip-Van-Winkle-
in-reverse process by which I could be taken back twenty
years, when Drake began to work toward its Doctor of Arts
program, but by which I could be intimately involved in that
work—even as department chair, if you want—and by which

I could be armed ahead of time with the foresight which, unfortunately, we never have in such matters—in other words with twenty years of hindsight before the fact. Based on such normally impossible awareness, what would I know, what key questions might I ask, what demands might I make, and what might my expectations be before venturing very far into such a program?

The principal thing I could expect—and indeed, it is so obvious that it seems to get overlooked all of the time— is for conditions surrounding the program's establishment to change, even radically. In most everything we do we never truly perceive the present; we can at best perceive only a recent past. This is why every academic program is in a sense necessarily obsolete at the time of its adoption. A prime example of changing conditions, which may receive considerable attention at this session, is the shift within many Ph.D. programs, at least in English, toward more preparation in pedagogy for candidates planning to teach. In the program out of which I graduated in the late 1960s, no formal attention whatsoever was given to preparing me as a teacher *per se*, and I doubt that it was unusual in that regard. Charles Silbermann a few years before that had observed that the relegation of teacher-preparation to often mindless education courses in teachers colleges and the like was the direct result of the liberal arts having abandoned their responsibility toward the training of teachers. Nothing confirms Silbermann's contention better than the assumption that somehow persons trained to do formal research and to publish in academic specialties will automatically learn to teach those specialties to undergraduates, and to teach them well. At any rate, the scandalous state of affairs which gave rise to various studies and reports and led to the beginning of the D.A. has changed to the extent that many Ph.D. programs routinely include pedagogical instruction and supervision in their candidates' training.

Relatedly, since the early 1970s composition has gained dramatically in stature as part of our discipline—with its own growing professional organizations, journals, research protocols, and inroads into territory once exclusively belonging to literature—including the English-language segment of the MLA itself. Because "composition," in fact, means the study of *teaching* composition—and because virtually all research in composition is pedagogical in nature and implication—the infiltration of composition specialists into departments of English and the growing interest of faculty members, even those not specializing in composition theory, has meant a necessary growth of attention to pedagogical issues in general. If literary study still lags far behind composition in terms of attending to such issues, if there are still all-too-few sessions at the MLA on teaching, there are now at least some, and the number is growing— it is no longer fashionable, as it probably was when I started my teaching career, to attack talk about pedagogy in literature as unacademic or otherwise bad form. And interestingly, composition theorists are succeeding much better than their literature counterparts in following the implications of post-structuralism and deconstructionism, those most extreme gestures of recent *literary* theory, in the classroom. In this they are leading the way and increasingly giving the lie to the still-prevalent attitude that composition represents a "soft option" among English programs: they are increasingly asking and responding to hard questions.

The point of this seeming digression is that some shift of emphasis has occurred throughout the profession, and even if far from completed—even if many English departments still stubbornly resist it, even if the tenuous place of writing teachers in the English department is still one of the scandals of the profession—it represents a profession-wide response to challenges issued by the Carnegie Corporation and others calling for educational reforms in the late 1960s. To the extent that the D.A. has contributed to this change of climate, to an accompanying reassessment of research and teaching priorities, and to making the traditional Ph.D. less traditional, it has diminished the philosophical advantage it once had and has thus benefited the profession in a way in which its founders at various institutions perhaps could not have envisioned or even desired.

Conditions do change, and they change in ways no one can predict. They change inside the institution, as well. Presidents and deans don't stay around indefinitely, or they do so at the peril of the institutions they serve. Their particular styles of leadership, their priorities, and their visions of the university, however persuasive at certain points in an institution's development, often leave with them, to be replaced by others. The administrative encouragement and resource support for a program at its inception can diminish or disappear, and quite quickly, to the extent that it depends on one or two key individuals. It seems wise to be aware of what such support means and does not mean, and to own up to the programmatic implications of key administrative changes when they occur. Relatedly, supporters in other departments, who see an advantage to them in the adoption of a program—perhaps a precedent from which they can follow their own ambitions—may, as time passes, alter those ambitions and their view of a particular program they once supported, and may even become its critics. I am not suggesting there is anything sinister or unprincipled in all of this: it is part of university politics which, because a programmatic decision is in part always a political decision, must be recognized, expected and even embraced as programmatic objectives are pursued. Similarly, the fiscal health of the institution, which can fluctuate widely, can constitute both a condition for beginning a graduate program and a reason to contain or even eliminate it.

Perhaps the most striking change of conditions, and that having the most direct bearing on a program, is change within the department itself. Like presidents and deans, professors move on, and others arrive. Departments, like families, contain generations, and one generation's agenda may not be the next's. I have already noted how non-planners become managers, how the spectators at the erecting of a program may in time become the persons principally responsible for it. Whether this argues for allowing no one to remain merely a spectator, or for making everyone a planner from the beginning, I am not sure. I am sure, though, that those doing the planning would be foolish not to expect considerable change in department personnel, and thus to regard, and in a sense respect, every present spectator as a potential future manager. Unquestionably, inviting junior faculty to participate in the planning process is to risk their raising objections and thus retarding that process--even wrecking it if their objections are sufficiently serious and persuasive. Such a risk may not be worth taking. However, there is an at-least equal risk in not inviting the opinions and participation of all, since the quiet and seemingly indifferent spectator may, in fact, have strong views and objections and may several years later find the courage and the appropriate forum for voicing them. (Tenure, I have observed, works as a marvelous elixir for bringing out latent opinions.) Of course, as in the experience I cited earlier, potential dissenters, by gradually becoming participants in the program once it is implemented, may modify their objections and become supporters. The point is that it is impossible to have things both ways with such people and that each way carries an attendant risk.

The final change I might expect is from comparative advantage to disadvantage. Just as a program may give a department stature or an advantageous position within the institution, that position can become its opposite as conditions change. Or, the arguments which initially gain such advantage may ultimately define disadvantage. If, for example, the adoption of a program is speeded by the argument that it is relatively inexpensive, that argument may turn against the department using it when, some time later, increased resources for the program are needed, for it may be viewed as a promise that the program will always be equally inexpensive. When resources are needed for such things as increased stipends for graduate assistants, the institution's reluctance to beef up such support can catch a department in a bind as it attempts to compete for first-rate candidates. Such developments can transform a program from a bright opportunity into a drag on department energy and resources, and can make other departments which never enjoyed such a seeming advantage appear relatively well off, because freer to pursue other interests and concerns.

A corollary to all that I have said—and perhaps its upshot— is that anyone responsible for establishing or maintaining an academic program such as the Doctor of Arts ought to monitor carefully what sort of motives are actually driving the program at any particular point in its history. Personally, I favor making programmatic changes for academic reasons— though vulnerable in that they are often (and by some, easily) cast aside, academic reasons have a wonderful way of bouncing back and thus transcending the narrower interests to which they sometimes fall prey. Even so, I am not so naive as to expect that some form of expediency will not intrude from time to time. With such an expectation, it becomes important to measure a program's health in terms of the reasons or motives which mean the most to the persons responsible for it, and not to mask expediency as somehow satisfying such reasons. It becomes important to face up to the *real* motives at work, to resist pressures to substitute a lesser rationale, and, when the gap between desirable motive and actual driving motive becomes too great, to admit and act on the implications of that gap.

Whether all of these principles were at work in the minds of those persons founding our doctoral program, I don't know—no doubt some were, though I never asked. And, whether I myself could keep them in mind under similar circumstances, I also do not know, though I hope so. They do seem important and worth remembering at all times.

REVIEW OF
NATIONAL LITERATURES

OICE

AY '85

nguage and
terature

ther

8

ARMENIA. special editor: Vahe Oshagan. Published for the Council on National
Literatures by Griffon House, 1984. 264p (Review of national literatures, 13)
77-126039. 40.00 ISBN 0-918680-20-0; 20.00 pa ISBN 0-918680-22-0

A rich, informative, and diverse collection by 11 specialists on Armenian and comparative literatures. The articles provide a comprehensive perspective of ancient, medieval,
modern, and Soviet Armenian literature and also focus on several key literary figures.
A. Paolucci begins the collection with the origins, growth, and development of Armenian literature and the various translations into Armenian of the best achievements of
Western literature. Other articles deal with the revival of Armenian literature in the
mid-19th century (Oshagan); the influence of Russian critical realism on the plays of
Soundoukian, Baronian, and Shirvanzade (Alexanian); the relationship between Armenian and other European literatures (Etmekjian); the principal themes of medieval
Armenian poets (Nersissian); the poets Tourian (Zekiyan) and Charents (Tamrazian);
the plays of Soundoukian, Baronian, Shirvanzade, Shant, and Demirjian (Hakhver-
dian); the efforts of Armenian writers to attain a cosmopolitan character in their works
(Oshagan); and Armenian literature in Armenian from the mid-19th century to recent
times (Nersessian). Finally, H. Paolucci and Parlakian review the critical assessments
of recent histories in English. This collection touches merely the surface of Armenian
literature; nevertheless, it is highly recommended to all interested in the literature of an
ancient culture and is appropriate for graduate students and upper-division undergraduates.—*I.D. Barooshian, Wells College*

Review of National Literatures

EDITOR: ANNE PAOLUCCI

STILL AVAILABLE . . . .

[SEMI-ANNUAL SERIES: 1970 — 1975*]

MACHIAVELLI '500
HEGEL IN COMPARATIVE LITERATURE *(Sp. Ed. Frederick G. Weiss)*
IRAN *(Sp. Ed. Javad Haidari)*
BLACK AFRICA *(Sp. Ed. Albert S. Gerard)*
RUSSIA: THE SPIRIT OF NATIONALISM *(Sp. Ed. Charles A. Moser)*
SHAKESPEARE AND ENGLAND *(Sp. Ed. James G. McManaway)*
TURKEY: FROM EMPIRE TO NATION *(Sp. Ed. Talat Sait Halman)*
THE FRANCE OF CLAUDEL *(Sp. Ed. Henri Peyre)*
THE MULTINATIONAL LITERATURE OF YUGOSLAVIA *(Sp. Ed. Albert B. Lord)*
GREECE: THE MODERN VOICE *(Sp. Ed. Peter Mackridge)*
CHINA'S LITERARY IMAGE* *(Sp. Ed. Paul K. T. Sih)*

[NEW ANNUAL SERIES: 1976 —]

CANADA *(Sp. Ed. Richard J. Schoeck)*
HOLLAND *(Sp. Ed. Frank J. Warnke)*
GERMAN EXPRESSIONISM *(Sp. Ed. Victor Lange)*
INDIA *(Sp. Ed. Ronald Warwick)*
AUSTRALIA *(Sp. Ed. L. A. C. Dobrez)*
NORWAY *(Sp. Ed. Sverre Lyngstad)*
ARMENIA** *(Sp. Ed. Vahe Oshagan)*
PIRANDELLO *(Sp. Ed. Anne Paolucci)*
COLUMBUS*** *(Sp. Ed. Henry Paolucci)*
JAPAN*** *(Sp. Ed. John Gillespie)*
COMPARATIVE LITERARY THEORY: AN OVERVIEW *(Sp. Ed. Anne Paolucci)*
HUNGARY*** *(Sp. Ed. Eniko Basa)*

Only one volume issued in 1975.
**Hardbound volume also available for $40.*
*** In preparation.*

ALL VOLUMES: $23 each; $US ONLY, PREPAID (P/H incl.)

TO ORDER: Send check and titles to CNL, P. O. Box 81

Whitestone, New York 11357.

Review of National Literatures

Editor: Anne Paolucci

COMING!!

COLUMBUS,

AMERICA, AND THE WORLD

Special Editors:
ANNE PAOLUCCI / HENRY PAOLUCCI

As part of its world-wide series, REVIEW OF NATIONAL LITERATURES, *the Council on National Literatures will issue in the Spring of 1987 a volume dedicated to Columbus from a literary/historical perspective. Contents include:*

Introduction: "Columbus and the Idea of America"

Frank J. Coppa: "Christopher Columbus and Italy"

John Gillespie: "Paul Claudel's *Christopher Columbus* and Japanese Noh Plays"

Marie-Lise Gazarian: "A Doer, A Dreamer and a Man of Vision"

O. Carlos Stoetzer: "The 'Myth' of Discovery: Edmundo O'Gorman's Perspective"

Dino Bigongiari: "Dante's Ulysses and Columbus" (edited by Henry Paolucci)

Foster Provost: "Christopher Columbus: A Bibliographical Spectrum"

LCCC: 77-126039   ISSN: 0034-6649